D0615488

A Teen-Ager's Guide to Personal Success

A Teen-Ager's Guide to Personal Success

ERMA PAUL FERRARI

ILLUSTRATED BY LEONARD REDDING

ABINGDON PRESS
NEW YORK NASHVILLE

A TEEN-AGER'S GUIDE TO PERSONAL SUCCESS

Library of Congress Catalog Card Number: 57-11010

C

SET UP, PRINTED, AND BOUND BY THE PARTHENON PRESS, AT NASHVILLE, TENNESSEE, UNITED STATES OF AMERICA

CONTENTS

1

You Are Important

SELF-IMPORTANCE, AS WE ORDINARILY understand the term, is not an attractive characteristic. Nobody admires a person who thinks he knows all the answers or who, even if he does in a given subject, toots his knowledge all over the place.

But there is a kind of self-importance that you should rate as high as your favorite form of athletics or social grace or the most coveted manual skill. It is the kind of self-importance that is based on such an appreciation of yourself as a person that you put an extremely high value on your life, refuse to settle for anything second rate, and determine to make the most of that very special and interesting person—you.

No matter what your background, where you live, how much or how little money you have, what your abilities are, *you* as an individual, apart from everyone else, are tremendously important. You should believe that very firmly. There are many reasons why it is true, and it is a fact easily proved. It "figures"!

In the first place, you are important because you are an original edition—different physically, mentally, and emotionally from any other person who ever lived on this earth or who ever will. And because you are different, you make a difference to yourself and to a lot of other people. You have a life that is your own to develop. No one else can do this for you. You are making now, and you will continue to make as long as you live, an impact on many people, beginning with your family, that no one else can make. They will be happier, stronger, more hopeful, or they will be sadder, weaker, less hopeful, because of *you*. In your own unique way you influence your school, your gang, your community, and someday your spot in the world of work, because you are you—different from anyone else.

You are also very important to some people you will never meet. Mass production in America has not reached the point where the individual is ignored by business, by the government, or by society in general. Quite the contrary. As a consumer you are of vital interest to business, which wants your patronage. As a citizen you will be of vital interest to the candidate for office, who wants your vote. As a worker, you will soon be very much the concern of employers, who must depend upon what you produce in goods or services.

Advertisers, political parties, social organizations, and pressure groups of all varieties spend millions to get your individual trade, attention, and support.

All this adds up to somebody pretty special. And why not? Come to think of it, a mighty big lot has gone into your production. From generations and centuries you have inherited things and skills and ideals that are more valuable to you than any amount of material wealth. Those clever prehistoric men who first put fire to use, or slowly and laboriously over the centuries developed the wheel, or discovered what seem to us commonplace physical laws, contributed priceless skills and knowledges to you. Those thinkers of ancient Greece who gave expression to mankind's first vague ideas about democratic living, those legal minds of ancient Rome, those craftsmen and writers and musicians and artists from every age and every land—all have helped immeasurably to build your life as you live it today in modern America. So, in the second place, you are important because of your inheritance. You as an individual are heir to a great and noble legacy, all the culture of the wonderful world in which you live. It is a thrilling idea that you may, through your own talents and abilities, add something to that culture or lift it to a higher level.

Finally, and above all other reasons, you are important as an individual because of your value in the sight of God, your creator. He gave you life and he will help you make the most of that life. Hundreds of thousands of people of every generation who have ventured forth, believing that they mattered a great deal to God and had some particular place to fill in his plan for life, have proved it, not through a blind, unquestioning faith, but through vital, sometimes amazing experience. Your life can have no higher motive or achieve no more triumphant goal than that—wherever you are and in whatever capacity—you serve God and through him your neighbor.

Look to Your Blueprints

Unless you were unusually clever, you would never think of building a cottage at the lake or making a smart dress without a blueprint or a pattern. You can't build the kind of *life* you want without a pattern either. You have only to look around you to prove to yourself that lives without plans, like buildings or garments without plans, are unattractive in design, wasteful of the materials that went into them, and turn out to be either completely useless or far from what they might have been. The "town bum" never planned to be the town bum. Twenty-five years ago he might have laughed at the idea or been horrified at it. But he drifted and built his life without a pattern. That high-strung socially successful woman never planned to go to pieces at fifty and look back over a career just about empty of anything worth remembering, but she had no pattern either and drifted along with her environment.

It is encouraging to know that young men and women living in America today can create just about any pattern for the future that they want to follow. It isn't always easy, and we all make mistakes in our building; but if you want very earnestly to be a special kind of person, the chances are good that you can be, provided you start now on your blueprints.

That pattern for your life must be based on three things: what you want as a finished product, what you have to work with, and the knowledge and experience of all those who have lived and built successfully before you. Let's talk about these three things for a bit.

Deciding upon the person you want to be, your "finished product," involves some daydreaming, by no means a waste of time if you don't overdo it. Most great people have laid plans for their lives in their dreams. They have pictured themselves building a bridge of strength and beauty, making a speech on the floor of the Senate, capturing applause on the concert stage, owning their own shop, serving a great church, breeding prize stock, planting wide acres, presiding over a home as wife and mother. Building such castles in the air is worth while provided, as Thoreau suggests, you then build foundations of reality under your castles. We shall have more to say later about that finished product—the person you want to be vocationally, socially, and spiritually.

What you have to work with starts, of course, with yourself. At this point in your career you may not think you stand out from your fellows as particularly clever, artistic, or mentally keen. You are just a garden-variety fellow or girl, nothing brilliant or startling or fancy. This may or may not be true, but the number of your assets—the tools you have in the way of personal equipment—may surprise you when you start taking an inventory of them. We'll search for those too, later. You may be sure that you have your share of tools to work with, including some you haven't yet discovered and others you can cultivate.

Fortunately you can bring into your building, skills and ideas from the vast store of the world's knowledge. You are doing just this when you tackle your homework; you are doing it when you engage in some sport, cultivate a hobby, read, travel, join the school orchestra or the debating society, tinker with the car, or listen to the advice of somebody who knows more about something than you do. In short, there is a deep reservoir of resources at your finger tips. Some of them were handed to you on a platter. A lot of them you will have to dig for as you create your pattern. That's the fun and the challenge of living.

One of the purposes of this book is to help along with your building. Young men and women like yourself helped to write it. Their interests, their failures, their problems, their successes, are all here to help you construct the blueprint for your own life. These young people believed they were important, that their lives were too valuable to waste or to handicap by getting off to a bad start.

The fact that thousands of fellows and girls have the same material and intellectual inheritance and much the same potential that you have does not alter the fact that you as an individual will make history. It may be good, bad, or indifferent history; but you will make it in your particular sphere of life, as they will make it in theirs. You are that important.

Few people know that the man who is now Poet Laureate of England once tramped the streets of an American city while looking for a job. But during the time that he searched and took anything he could find in the way of work, even washing dishes in a cheap restaurant for a period, he kept his eye on the blueprint he was creating. He believed in himself and in the plan he had for his life. Rough times, rugged going, rubbing elbows with all kinds of people—taking no experience for granted, but making use of them all—built a great poet. And the day came not long ago when his queen, addressing the people of the British Commonwealth all over the world, quoted some inspiring lines that this great poet, John Masefield, had once written to youth:

> Though you have conquered Earth and chartered Sea
> And planned the courses of all Stars that be,
> Adventure on, more wonders are in thee.
> Adventure on, for from the littlest clue
> Has come whatever worth man ever knew.
> The next to lighten all men may be you.[1]

[1] "The Ending," COLLECTED POEMS, copyright 1930, 1951. Used by permission of The Macmillan Company.

2

Starting with What You Have

TAKE A LONG LOOK IN THE MIRROR one of these days and reflect on what you see there. Concentrate for a much longer period of time than it ordinarily takes to apply your lipstick or tie your four-in-hand.

What you see in your mirror are some of the things that you have been given for free. You neither chose them nor earned them. But they are to be reckoned with very seriously, for they are your working tools, the things you will use in creating that person you hope to be.

Of course, some of the things your mirror reflects back at you do not matter too much—the shape of your nose or the color of your eyes. But many of the things *behind* those eyes matter a great deal—your temperament, your disposition, your intelligence. You had no choice about these gifts either. You had nothing to say about that stubborn streak you inherited from Dad's "side of the house" or the clever pair of hands you were lucky enough to pull out of fate's big hat. But you have a great deal to say about what you *do* with these gifts. If you are smart, you are going to use all of them—your appearance;

your personality; your mentality; yes, even your stubborn streak; in short, your complete equipment—to build your life.

When you turn away from the mirror and look about you, you see other things that were not of your own choosing, but which are also very much a part of you. The family and home into which you were born; the community environment in which you have spent your life thus far; the period of the world's history into which you came, with all the advantages, the fears, the demands that this age brings to you.

All these conditions and situations you were plopped down into. And most of them are pretty wonderful, by and large. You sometimes wake up in the morning quietly happy or all a-tingle with *joie de vivre,* as your French teacher would say. Of course, a few of your legacies you would like to change, or so you think at the moment—straight hair that won't hold a permanent or the home town where "nothing ever happens." But even hair can be managed, and someday the home town will look pretty good and then you'll wonder what you ever griped about.

But let's get back to the mirror and its reflection, for this is where you start on your blueprint—in other words, with your personal appearance. Despite all the old chestnuts about appearances being deceptive and clothes not making the man, your appearance *is* tremendously important, for it is what everybody sees first. Before they know anything about what is underneath, about the real you, they have only your personal appearance to judge you by.

When an advertising agency gets a new customer account, its staff members spend time and money deciding what medium they will use to publicize their customer's product. Shall it be TV, radio, newspapers, magazines? Your personal appearance is your own advertising medium. It's worth spending some time on. If a young fellow much in need of a haircut slouches down the street, is anyone encouraged to think that he has something on the ball, that his mind is alert to the interesting world about him? Is his medium selling him to advantage? If a girl's skirt could do with a pressing, what prospective employer would infer that here is a trim, smart secretary in the making?

Yes, personal appearances do matter very much, even though you may have other things with high ratings, such as intellect or character, to offer. Interviewers for jobs, college entrance examiners, acquaintances who would make interesting friends, teachers who must recommend you—all have a right to assume that untidy habits reflect a disorderly mind, that careless grooming marks an irresponsible person. This may not be true, but the observer is tempted to think so, and he usually has no time or inclination to dig deeper to discover how bright, capable, and reliable you really are. All of us turn away from the unattractive person and give our attention to the next in line who is well turned out.

Now, like most young people, you very likely have some complaints about your appearance. You are too tall or too short, too fat or too thin. Your hair is straight, fine, and unmanageable. Your nose is too large, your eyes are pale in color, and so on. These are annoyances. They have high nuisance value, but they are not problems, because you can do something about them. In short, you can be an attractive person if you care enough to work at it. I am thinking right now of one of the greatest actresses in America. She is neither pretty nor beautiful, according to ordinary standards of beauty. But she has a lot of other qualities that do more for her than beauty alone, as they will for you: good posture, a clear complexion, a becoming hairdo, a sincere smile, alert eyes, the right clothes, and her own particular talent. She took what nature gave her and built on it to become a charming, creative artist who brings audiences to their feet in admiration. This artist happens to be a woman, but a young man does not need a classical profile or the physique of a football tackle to be a personable, good-looking fellow and therefore make the right impression on everyone he meets. And this is just as necessary for a boy as for a girl. Fortunately some of your worries are simply the physical result of growth and body changes. Teen-age glands sometimes cut up puzzling capers and create blemishes. But the chances are these will disappear in a few years or so, with help on your part. Unclear skin and over- or underweight can often be remedied with proper diet, enough sleep, exercise out of doors, and rigid habits of cleanliness.

Height is another common concern, especially of young men. If you are worried about your pint size, it may well be that in a couple of years or so you will take a spurt and grow taller fast. If, on the other hand, you grew tall earlier than most of your pals, they may catch up with you before long. Because girls usually mature before boys of the same age, a girl of sixteen may be taller, even larger, than boys of her age, and both are uncomfortable together. But the boys are usually ahead at the finish. Not that it matters much, in the light of all the other attractions that both young men and young women have to offer.

During these years of rapid growth, you may find your body, or parts of it, unmanageable. Hands and feet get in the way, and you feel clumsy. You have probably said and done the wrong thing many times just from sheer awkwardness, leaving you in a worse spot than before! Well, cheer up. One of these days you will discover that you are once more in the driver's seat and that hands and feet are doing your bidding.

Whatever your particular form of "growing pain," do what you can to control it, ignore what cannot be helped right now, dig into your homework, cultivate a hobby just for kicks, improve those tennis and swimming strokes, or have some sessions with the piano you have been neglecting, and thus draw your own and other people's attention away from what you may think is a physical drawback. Make the most of what you have.

Far more important than the size and shape of the mold that nature poured you into is your health, for a healthy body is basic to good looks and radiates an attractive personality. You are fortunate to be growing up in this day when much is known about disease prevention and health habits that keep our bodies strong. So let your good health work for you, and do all you can to preserve it. Here are some quickies for your guidance. If you break these rules too often, you are headed for trouble sooner or later.

1. Get eight to ten hours of sleep every night, with rare exceptions like a big date or some other important event. You have had enough sleep if you wake up in the morning feeling rested, cheerful, and hungry! All are equally important. If you are easily fatigued, don't be ashamed to take a rest period of five minutes or so during the day. This rids the body of the wastes that have created your fatigue.

2. Eat three wholesome meals a day, at regular hours. Vegetables, fruit, milk, and high-protein foods like meat and eggs are musts for a strong, healthy body and a clear complexion. Sweets are okay in moderate quantities, provided you watch their effect on your teeth. You need some sugar for more bounce per ounce. But if you find that chocolate creates pimples

and that too many sessions at the drugstore are adding pounds to an already chubby figure, confine your snacks to fruit juice. But remember, dieting does not mean fasting. Unless you are seriously overweight or are gaining year by year, you can eat normally and let Mother Nature take her own good time in carving out the right figure for you.

To help you watch those snacks and that nibbling between meals, the table below gives you the caloric value of some of your favorites. A calorie, as of course you know, is a unit used to measure the heat value of food. The higher the caloric value of food, the more energy it gives you. But if you eat more than you need for body repair and energy, the waistline will start to expand. So—if you are seriously overweight:

Your Enemies!	
Coca Cola—1 cup	100 cals.
Chocolate milk—1 cup	200 cals.
Coffee cake—average	200 cals.
Milk shake, with ice cream	600 cals.
Candy bar	250 cals.
Ice cream, plain vanilla—1 cup	400 cals.
Chocolate—1 cup	500 cals.
Ice-cream soda	300 cals.
Hot fudge sundae	400 cals.
Peanuts—9	100 cals.
Potato chips—9	100 cals.
Peanut butter—1 tablespoon	100 cals.

Your Friends!	
Milk—1 cup	166 cals.
Lemonade—1 cup	75 cals.
Tomato juice—1 cup	50 cals.
Bran muffin—1 medium	75 cals.
Rye crisps—2	50 cals.
Shredded wheat biscuit, with milk	125 cals.
Pretzels—6	50 cals.
Apple—1 average	100 cals.
Banana—1 average	100 cals.
Egg, boiled or poached	70 cals.

You can help yourself along by gradually changing your eating habits. In fact, that is pretty much the whole trick.

If you are seriously underweight, pay a visit to the doctor and do as he tells you to. He will probably encourage you to butter your bread generously, drink plenty of milk, treat yourself to milk shakes, and include in your lunch sandwiches of peanut butter, jelly, and cheese. And ice cream is for you! How your chubby friends envy you, so congratulate yourself and reach for a second helping!

3. Get some outdoor exercise every day. This will tone up your muscles and keep your organs in good working order. Choose your own form of exercise though, one that you like and that is suited to your needs. If you tire easily, don't tackle anything too strenuous. A workout with the punching bag may be okay for Jim, but you might profit more from a group activity, such as volleyball or a hike.

4. Pass up the stimulants tea, coffee, and "pep" pills, in favor of milk, hot chocolate, fruit juice, or harmless soft drinks; and avoid the depressants alcohol and drugs in any form—they lead to serious trouble. Do not become an early tobacco addict, either, and lose both your wind and your freedom.

5. See to it that your teeth are kept in good repair, even if you have to baby-sit or get some other part-time job to pay for it.

6. Keep your emotions under control. Make them work *for* your good health and not against it. We'll hear some interesting things later about these complicated feelings of ours. But remember now that a pleasant emotion brings you added physical and mental strength. Unpleasant emotions have the opposite effect. Fortunately, there are ways of getting these unruly ones by the scruff of the neck and demonstrating who is boss.

It's fun to be fit. Much of your success and happiness depends upon good health. But there are other aspects of an attractive appearance that cannot be neglected either. Here they are.

Cleanliness. A daily scrubbing with soap and water will give you a clean, healthy sparkle that no amount of cosmetics can supply. And speaking of cosmetics—remember, girls—they were really invented to camouflage the aging process. If you use them too heavily, you will cover up the very things that cosmetics attempt to create for the oldsters. So if lipstick is sure to start an argument at the breakfast table, it may not be worth it—no more than a dash anyway.

Try the soap-and-water routine for those pimples and blackheads. They require a gentle scrubbing with a good lather. A tub or a shower does something for you inside too. You step out not only clean, but also invigorated and pepped and poised. Fellows sing or whistle in the shower and girls get relaxed in the tub because of this pleasant mental and physical reaction.

Good grooming. Hair must be clean, brushed, and combed. Girls who wear their hair long must be especially attentive to its condition. The one-hundred-strokes-a-day rule is recommended, if your hair is not overly oily. If it is, so much brushing will make it more so. Coarse, wiry hair profits from the use of an after-shampoo rinse and a small amount of hairdressing or a light spray of lacquer. There is no danger that you will wash your hair too much. City dwellers may need to shampoo every few days. And every girl needs a trip to the beauty parlor once in three months or so for shaping and thinning those locks. Be cautious about bleaching those "lucky streaks" into your hair, for it grows at the rate of about one-half inch a month, and the streaks will be with you for a long time! And boys, don't ruin the natural shade of your hair and its normal texture by applying greasy ointments or "plastering" it down unnaturally with water.

Shoes, when not on rough or sport duty, should be polished. School and social clothes should be clean and pressed. Nails should be filed and not ragged from nervous biting or smudged with pealing nail polish.

Straight posture. Just to throw your shoulders back and lift your head heightens your own opinion of yourself. Try it and see. And it certainly gives others the impression that you have poise and self-control. If you think you are too tall, don't make the bad mistake of slumping to decrease your height. You will only develop ugly round shoulders and throw your body into strange angles. Walk straight and tall, with natural grace. If you are short, good posture will pull you up and make you look taller than you actually are. For both tall and short, becoming designs and colors in clothes will work miracles. So, here we go!

3

"What Shall I Wear?"

ALL THE FUSS AND BOTHER THAT fashion sometimes seems to demand did not just happen. The fact is that there are interesting aspects to personal dress that make the difference between being becomingly and fashionably dressed and merely protected from the elements. Basically, fashion, whether found in the masculine or feminine world, is the result of our desire to present ourselves as special, distinct individuals, to express our own personalities. While we work at getting our figures, complexions, and other physical evidences of our personality into condition, we can make our clothes work for us too.

There are two basic principles to be followed in the wise selection of clothes:

1. My clothes should do something special for *me*. They should complement my physical appearance and express some basic personality pattern.

2. My clothes should be in keeping with my day-to-day life; in other words, they should be appropriate to the kinds of things I do.

The nearer one can come to these two objectives, the better

he will be dressed. Of course, too much stress on one or the other of these two objectives can make for some pretty odd concoctions. For instance, it might be a little awkward for a girl to appear at her office job in lurid clothes chosen to express the "gypsy" tendencies that everybody feels on occasions, especially in the spring, or to dash to classes decked out as a mysterious international spy. These farfetched examples illustrate the need for balance and discretion in selecting clothes that express your true personality.

Well, then, how do you go about choosing clothes that will do something for you, a teen-ager in high school? Let's concentrate on the girls' problem first.

Your main concern (with a limited amount of money, of course) will be to select a piece of wearing apparel that will bear up under a bit of strain, but also something that you can wear to school fairly frequently without getting bored with it. A suit or a dark dress will usually fill that particular bill, but not *just* a suit or just *any* dark dress. This suit or dress must be a pivot for the rest of your wardrobe to revolve around.

In selecting this very special suit or dress, let's take a cool look in that mirror again, for your choice is going to depend a good deal on whether you are short or tall, very slender or on the chubby side, on the shade of your complexion, and so on. Almost nobody is completely satisfied with her physical characteristics, but this is where one uses her head and meets the challenge. And this often means playing up what at first might seem like a really detracting characteristic and transforming it into an asset.

The first consideration in our choice is *line*. Line is as important as color or material, if not more so. Remember that no matter how happy your color selection or choice of style, if a suit or a dress does not fit across the shoulders, pulls a little here and there, is too long- or short-waisted, it is not your suit or dress. Its lines are not yours. Incidentally, if you have trouble fitting into ready-made sizes, always include the charge for alterations in your total cost. There are horizontal lines in garments, wrap-around lines, slim lines, flared lines, and many others in the wide variety of styles available to you today. And here are a few hints in selecting the particular lines that will be becoming to you.

If you are inclined to be plump as well as tall, affectionately known as a "big girl," look for a suit or dress with natural shoulder lines rather than padded. Perhaps a raglan shoulder line would be your best choice. You will do well also to choose a straight or semi-fitted jacket rather than a fitted one. This means that you are concentrating on the unbroken line and subtle grace. And in keeping with this idea of grace—and *you* can be graceful as well as the petites—remember to wear shoes with moderate heels. The few inches they add to your height will be far preferable to the ungainly appearance created by "flats."

Avoid rough, heavy tweeds, mannish styles, and splashy prints or figures in dress materials. But at the same time, do not choose very delicate or tiny accessories, such as small jeweled earrings or postage-stamp hats. These are entirely out of harmony with your figure. On the other hand, accessories that other girls would love to carry or wear, but can't—large purses made of interesting leathers; strong, even exotic jewelry; and sometimes most unusual hats—are perfect for you. You can "carry" such, and tiny girls cannot. Of all figure problems, yours provides the greatest opportunity for unusual touches, but not too many at a time. Do not be afraid of your size; but remember, as you select your clothes, the graceful dignity and poise of the classic Grecian and Roman beauties.

A few tricks will also help to lengthen and slim down the silhouette of the short, plump figure. If this description fits you, you will look for clothes that are graceful but not overpowering. You will pass by the broken line that creates the illusion of weight: for example, a suit with one color predominating in the jacket and another color in the skirt, or one that uses a contrasting shade at the waist- or hipline. You do not want shoulders that are heavily padded either, or those that slope radically. Look for a smooth but definite shoulder line, a semi-fitted jacket rather than a form-fitting jacket. Select one that hits just below the waistline or at the top of the hip line, not one that spans the widest part of the hips. The most flattering skirts are those that flow from the waist, perhaps gored or flared, but not gathered.

Your hats and purses should match or complement the color of your clothes. It will be best to avoid a vivid contrast that will lessen the illusion of height that you want to create. Remember, too, that a wool jersey blouse or sweater of the same color as your suit will give a slimmer, taller line than a contrasting white blouse, that has a tendency to add pounds and cut height.

Because you are stockily built, you need not be afraid of those little touches that will set a style to your clothes—a lovely bracelet or pretty shoes; and for dress, always immaculate gloves. One does not need to be petite to be feminine. Cultivate warmth and gentleness—two qualities that will more than offset the disadvantages of being a little on the heavy side.

And now for the girl who may be tall and thin, and more or less constantly frustrated because an otherwise perfect dress is not only too short-waisted, but also ends just below the knees!

Unless you are very, very thin, a straight jacket can be flattering. And a classic jacket or one that is a full three-quarter length may be your happy choice. Be wary of tight jackets combined with straight skirts. This combination can produce an awkward, stick-like effect. However, remember that in your case the white blouse or contrasting sweater is flattering. No stripes, though.

If you are exceptionally thin and find straight skirts unflattering, look for pleated or gathered skirts. A box-pleated or accordion-pleated skirt, combined with a semifitted or full double-breasted jacket of medium length, is fine for you.

You will avoid extreme accessories, but do not be afraid of contrasting shades in bags, gloves, etc. Soft elegance is what you want, and not frills. And remember, bright cummerbunds and full peasant blouses show you off to fine advantage.

The slim, short gal has her problems too. Every dress, every skirt, has to be shortened and thus the line of the garment usually ruined, and the result is too often a curious, boxlike effect. To add to her dilemma, the short, slim girl is confronted with styles in her size that are babyish and too "cute." However, designers are becoming more realistic and are finally producing clothes with the very small girl in mind.

Actually, aside from inconvenience, the short, slim girl has many advantages. To produce an illusion of height, stick to matching or complementary colors in choosing an outfit. Avoid a skimpy appearance by emphasizing fullness. For instance, in selecting our make-believe suit, try a full skirt combined with a short, form-fitting jacket. Look for a full, soft collar and small French cuffs.

A word of caution—never buy clothes that are skin tight! Too often these create a skimpy, starved effect. Also, watch out for heavy tweeds that lose you somewhere in the weave! Instead, look for clothes with definite lines and crispness of style. Pert hats with high crowns; starched, sparkling white cotton blouses; crinoline petticoats under full skirts, are all fun and flattering to you. But be cautious about mixing colors. Try to match or complement them. Otherwise your small figure and your individuality will be lost in a polyglot of colors. Don't be afraid of bright colors, though, by themselves. If colors are selected with an eye to your shade of hair and skin, they can mark you as a person of importance, despite your lack of size.

More about *color*. What seasoning is to food, color is to clothes. Too much or too little, or a poor selection, can be as bad or worse than none at all. But do not let those dangers prevent you from experimenting with color. Choosing color can be fun and not too expensive. Scarves, ties, hairbands, even sweaters and blouses, do not make too big a dent in the clothes allowance. And a sense of color can remake a basic piece of apparel that you are very tired of.

No one color will work the same way for everybody. Nor can it generally be said of any color that it cannot be worn by certain people; so much depends on personal combinations of hair and skin tones. Although you may be ready to swear by your last breath that you cannot wear yellow, there may well be some untried shades of yellow that are not only wearable for you, but also flattering.

Keeping this in mind, there are a few general suggestions that may be helpful in carrying out your experimentations with color.

Fair-skinned blondes should try dark blues and greens to emphasize their fairness. The several lovely pastels are almost always becoming too. If you are unusually pale, a small white touch at the neckline will prevent these darker shades from swallowing you up.

Blondes with darker complexions must exercise a little caution. Watch out for shades that tend to emphasize any yellowish cast in your skin. Most flattering are rich tones of green, red, and blue, as well as some subtle, off shades of these colors, depending upon individual differences.

Redheads are often too conservative in their color choices. Various shades of green and blue are flattering; but with a little thought about skin tones, colors such as pink, brown, and even yellow may be worn with pleasantly surprising results. Red is the one color best avoided.

For *brown-haired beauties* there are many choice color combinations. But let your skin tones play a determining part. For example, a green that is flattering to your hair might play havoc with your complexion, and emphasize its yellow or gray undertones. Bright colors you may use with some splash—strong reds and clear blues and greens.

Brunettes with fair skin can highlight this nice contrast by wearing pastels or dark shades of blue, green, and red. Watch out for prints, though, which have a tendency toward a nondescript effect—one contrast canceling out the other.

Brunettes with deeper or olive skin tones can create exciting results with off shades of blue and red. Creamy whites, if chosen carefully, can be very effective for you.

Girls who have to wear glasses really get a break these days, so if you need them, don't leave them off and develop ugly wrinkles between your eyes or a horrible squint, and maybe ruin your eyesight in the bargain.

Frames for glasses are smart. They "do something" for you, and they may be worn almost like an accessory. Their colors and shapes often add to, rather than detract from, one's appearance. So select a color that is becoming to you, having in mind the shades of your hair and of your complexion, and a shape that is not too extreme, but one that flatters your face. If the lenses that you need are not too expensive, you might save your allowance and have two sets of frames, one for daytime and one for social events, of colors that match the outfits you wear oftenest.

And now, the boys. As a matter of fact, you fellows might scan through the notes given above on color and apply these principles to your selections of sweaters and ties and shirts. As with girls, splashy colors will add to the overweight fellow's handicap, but he can flaunt as bold a necktie as he likes. Tall fellows should usually avoid stripes. Sharp distinctions between jacket and trousers will be flattering. Shorter fellows can flaunt modest stripes, or a solid color for both jacket and trousers—which will add height.

It is not feminine to match your ties with your eyes and hair. It is smart grooming. But if you are a wonderful redhead, don't select a red tie. Make it harmonize with your brown, gray, or blue eyes. Let the salesman (and be sure he knows his business) advise you about the color of your suit. Don't buy navy blue, in spite of the "picture yourself in blue" ads, if you look better in brown, as many fellows do.

Avoid colors that you will soon tire of and that soil easily—light blue trousers, for example. Such colors are likely to be cheap-looking too. You will always find it rewarding to save your money for a time until you are able to pay a reasonable price for suits. Men's clothes, more than girls', have an appearance of quality, good or bad, and they cannot usually be camouflaged with clever lines to look better than they are.

Boys can have a wonderful fling with sweaters. Once again, watch your choice of colors, and keep that sweater spotlessly clean. A soiled sweater (when you are not engaged in rough work, of course) is just as repelling on a fellow as it is on a girl.

Your haircut is important, and don't wear a crewcut or any other style unless it becomes you. Ask advice of the barber or even of the favorite girl friend.

Always remember that there is no price tag on good taste. Although boys have an easier time of it clotheswise, they too must be dressed appropriately. Arriving at a party "all dressed up" and finding the other guests in casual clothes is somewhat painful. It is equally embarrassing to overdress at school or not to dress in respectful fashion for church. Find out what clothes you should wear and when to wear them. Fashions vary in different communities and from year to year. Sweaters, slacks, dungarees, evening wear, and tuxedoes all have their places. Boys, find out from the haberdasher what is proper for formal or semiformal dress. Current magazines are also a wonderful help for both fellows and girls. You will look good and feel at ease if you know you are dressed becomingly and appropriately for the occasion, be it picnic, school, party, or church. Take the time to dress properly, and then forget your appearance. A girl who self-consciously fusses with her hair or dress, or a fellow who nervously fingers his tie or his coat sleeves, spoils the most carefully planned appearance. You have dressed at home. Now turn your attention outward, to those about you. At this point, personality enters and takes over.

4

You Want to Belong

NOT LONG AGO A TELEVISION PLAY about a lonely young man created such unusual interest that it was bought for the movies. The script obviously "had something." The movie, too, was a hit all over the country and received important awards.

The reason for all this popularity was easy to explain. As they watched the screen, thousands of TV and movie spectators saw themselves in the leading role or in one very much like it. This shy young man wanted a nice girl to date, but he never seemed to be able to attract such a girl. In social situations he was likely to do and say the wrong things. "Whatever it is girls like, I haven't got it," he said to his mother one dateless night. So his evenings were boring and lonely—until he met a girl who was in something of the same fix.

At one time or another and in one form or another, this has been almost everybody's experience. No wonder the movie was popular.

There are some cruel words in the vocabulary of your generation—words like "dog," "chicken," "drip." The psychiatrists have professional terms to describe these types: "introverts," "insecure," "maladjusted"; but the meanings are the same. You would rather have almost anything happen than to be known as a "dog" among your associates. Above all things, you don't want to be different, ignored, or left out. You want to belong, to fit with some group, to be liked, to make friends, to have dates. And you know that the answer to your problem is in large measure a question of personality.

If only there were some formula like those you learn in chemistry: $H^2+O=$Personality. But whatever it is that makes us liked by and attractive to people is so much more complicated than chemistry! Personality is vague, many-sided, and hard to put your finger on. You cannot describe it accurately. You can just point to somebody and say, "He has personality." And everybody knows what you mean.

But let's see if we can be more helpful than that, for with all its vagueness, an attractive personality does include certain definite qualities. You find them in fellows and girls who are popular and liked by just about everybody.

Before we get at those characteristics, it may be helpful to get rid of some false notions that some of us may have about what an attractive personality is or how it is acquired.

First, personality is not necessarily noisy. The "life of the party" may, to be sure, be a popular fellow or girl who is just naturally lively. But he or she also may be a bore or a nuisance or a performer who puts on an act to cover up embarrassment and lack of social graces or to attract attention. Contrariwise, the quiet person may be attractive, good fun, and very generally well liked. And he is likely to wear a lot longer than the flashy performer. It is not necessary to break into any gathering with a splash. In fact, it is usually much better not to, especially if you have to put on an unnatural pose.

Second, personality and popularity cannot be bought with treats, or party-giving, or having a car to drive, or spending money lavishly. The boy with a car may be "used" for his car and therefore never lack for companions, but it is the car that attracts, not his personality. The car is a crutch that won't always be there. And the girl who treats at the drugstore or always insists on bringing or doing more than her share is not buying personality; she is being an easy mark whom everybody sees through. You can and should do some things to build an attractive personality, but what you do must have substance and must be based on what goes on inside you, not on forced behavior or material things.

Third, personality cannot be bought at the beauty parlor or at the cosmetic counter. "She's popular, she's pretty, she pampers herself with vanishing cream" reads fine in an ad, but the first two items are *not* the result of any cream or soap or lotion. It is important to be personally attractive; and a smart and becoming hairdo or haircut, a clear complexion, sound teeth, and the right clothes will help along. But personality includes these things, *plus*.

Fourth, personality is not acquired by trying to be like somebody else or copying somebody you admire, except in small doses. You will only end up by being a poor imitation. If you envy Jane and Bill their popularity, it's smart to study their personalities. Then you will do well to be as friendly and companionable as they are, but in your own style, not in theirs. Apple pie cannot parade as cream puffs, or cream puffs as apple pie, but they are both good desserts. Your personality may be quite unlike that of Jane or Bill, but it can be just as attractive. Be yourself and behave naturally.

Fifth, personality does not depend entirely upon the gifts

of nature, such as good looks, physical grace, or perfect features. Those are requirements for a modeling agency, but they might leave the home-town gang completely cold unless there were other items in the package. Disfigurements or physical handicaps have little effect on a personality which glows from within.

Finally, personality is not acquired by lowering one's standards or running around with the wrong crowd. It's no fun to sit at home when other girls are having dates or to be left out when you know the fellows are planning a "big" week end at the lake, but it is infinitely worse to "buy" dates with cheap lovemaking or invitations with behavior that leaves a bad taste in your mouth. And more important, it gets you nowhere. Dates and parties can be wonderful fun, or they can be cheapening, bitter experiences that let you down with a sickening thud. There are other ways to build your personality, to become popular, to have fun, to belong to a gang with the same standards as yours.

We all know that personality has many parts, each contributing something to make us attractive to others. As we consider some of these, one by one, let's keep in mind the following statement about personality. Would you agree that this is true? *Personality is the outward expression of the spirit within a person.* Read that line over again and think about it for a bit. It will help you to see how the qualities we are going to consider fit in.

First of all, attractive, popular people are *friendly*. They like people and let them know it, sometimes just by smiling and being pleasant when that is all that is called for. They are good listeners, too, and offer a sympathetic ear. Without forcing or overdoing it, they are helpful to others in many little ways.

Of course, standing around with a fixed smile isn't any help in breaking into a new group. In an embarrassing situation like that, it's a good idea to find something to do that will help along. One girl we know, invited to a party in a new community, was left stranded because of the negligence of the group, which should have planned differently. But this girl was resourceful. She found her way to the kitchen where refreshments would be coming up and she offered to help. Back in the kitchen is the spot where things are really going on, and she made friends at once, for girls get pretty chummy stacking dishes. She had other possibilities too for getting out of her "fix." She might have gone to the person who seemed to be in charge of the affair and asked to be introduced to another new guest. Or she might have brought a pal along with her to the party. Be resourceful and you can cope with almost any situation.

There is another way to be friendly and find friends in a strange group. Look about you for somebody else who seems to be alone and speak to him. Have his situation in mind instead of your own, and you have broken the ice for yourself and someone else as well.

Whatever your dilemma in a new group, don't get panicky. Even sitting or standing alone for a few minutes is not a painful experience if you interest yourself with ease and self-assurance in watching what is going on. Then when a game starts, join the circle; or carry your refreshments to a nearby group and quietly sit near. Don't force yourself upon them, but don't be afraid to pay a compliment, ask a question, or offer to help. And don't be crushed by an unfriendly snub, should one be forthcoming. In almost any group there are likely to be a few girls or fellows who feel so insecure themselves that they like to try to make someone else feel small. But don't let such a one use you to build up his own faltering ego. Ignore unfriendly slights and turn your attention elsewhere. Rarely are the majority of young people in any group unfriendly. If they are, they are not worth your time anyway.

The possible exception to the general rules for breaking into a new group is at a dance. Finding oneself a wallflower is a painful experience. If you learn to dance very well, that is not likely to occur. But if you have discovered that dancing is not your forte and that school dances, for example, are at best an unpleasant ordeal, you have two choices. First, ask for some task at the dance, such as tending the refreshment table, that will keep you occupied and at the same time keep you with the crowd, or accept the fact that dances are not your dish and turn your attention to those activities that *are,* those which will bring you just as many or more friends and fun. We'll get to that later.

Second, personable people are *kind,* and their kindness takes many forms. They show appreciation and speak generously of others. They hand out sincere compliments, not dishonest flattery. They don't try to build themselves up by running other people down. They are loyal and kind and make good companions. They are not overly sensitive and consequently always getting their feelings hurt. They are pleasant and cheerful. And remember, cheerful fellows and girls are not those with fewer troubles than other people; they are the ones who talk about them less and manage to look pleasant even though they are worried sick about the math test coming up or even something much more serious. Cheerfulness is a habit, just as being a sad sack is a habit. You can cultivate either, and there's no argument about which type of person you prefer to have around.

We have hinted above at some of the blocks to a friendly personality: oversensitivity, boasting, making unkind remarks. Being too possessive is another one. Just because Alice and

Peggy live on the same street and have played and studied together since fifth grade doesn't mean that Peggy may not accept an invitation to spend a week end at a friend's cottage without Alice. But you would think so from the way Alice behaved when she heard about it, for Alice has not grown up emotionally. She is childishly possessive, like a baby with a toy.

Being thoughtless and inconsiderate is the opposite of possessiveness, but it is just as fatal to personality-building and popularity. Inconsiderate fellows and girls keep pals waiting beyond the time set for meeting, push ahead of others in the cafeteria line, fail to write thank-you notes, ignore older people, shirk a committee or other group responsibility, forget a promise and leave someone in a spot, break a date for something that looks like more fun. A long list, but you could add more of these sure-fire ways *not* to be popular.

Perhaps you try to be friendly and kind but still feel that you don't "click." You find it hard to make friends, especially in new environments or situations. Or you would like to start with a clean slate in your home school and community, improve your personality, and make yourself more interesting and attractive to others.

That word *"interesting"* gives us our third clue. Instead of concentrating on yourself and the impression you are making, focus your attention on things you like to do, on favorite hobbies or on some activity that might become a hobby, on a skill you would like to cultivate, on a form of music or other art, on the school paper or on the dramatics club. If some of these activities are not available in your school or community, try to start something going yourself: a folk-dancing group; an orchestra, however small; a dramatics club; a community project.

Such an activity will accomplish several things. First, it will broaden your own interests and thus make you a more interesting, attractive person; it will turn your attention outward, away from yourself; it will give you poise and make you less self-conscious; and it will bring you new friends, for friendships that are worth while are almost always the by-products of mutual interests.

The possibilities for these aids to personality-building through activities and skills are almost limitless. A young man who appeared to be shy, almost diffident, had no social problem when it was discovered that he was an amateur magician of no mean talent. And a girl who can handle a tennis racket with dexterity, especially if she is willing to give some time to help poorer players with their strokes, is doing something for herself besides playing a smooth game of tennis. You see, such skills demand your concentration on things outside yourself. They are opening wedges to new acquaintances and broader experiences. They give you something to talk about on occasions that otherwise might prove difficult, and they also give other people a means of approach to *you*. All of us like attention. That is a legitimate desire. If we don't get it through some worth-while accomplishment, we are tempted to seek it through forced and unbecoming behavior that is fatal to personality-building.

Use your leisure time (oh, yes, you *do* have some) to cultivate a hobby that will add to your knowledge and interests and thus to your social accomplishments. But don't just grab any hobby out of the air. If you select one carelessly, you may get tired of it because it does not interest you or discouraged with it because it is beyond your abilities. Here are some pointers for selecting the right hobby for you:

1. You should like your hobby or at least feel rather certain that it will interest you.

2. You should be capable of it if it demands a definite skill or aptitude. You may, for example, surprise yourself with a paint brush; but on the other hand, you may have no artistic talents at all. So accept your limitations, physical or mental, and do not select a hobby that calls for something you just do not possess.

3. Your hobby should meet a need. If you need to know more about something, perhaps your hobby should be collecting. If you need social skill, your hobby should be something you can share with a group some day, such as a musical skill, square dancing, playing chess.

4. You should be able to afford your hobby, financially. Collecting antiques is expensive business. So is traveling. But you can collect something less expensive or confine your travels to the home environment and learn something about it historically, for example, and still ride your hobby.

5. You should have the time for it. Fortunately most hobbies in which young people are interested can be adapted to one's leisure, but becoming proficient at the piano takes a lot more time than woodworking or collecting activities.

All the above means simply that you should use good judgment in selecting your hobby and see to it that it fits you and your way of life.

Fourth, fellows and girls whom you would describe as having personality are genuinely *interested in other people*. These may be new acquaintances or old friends, but new or old, they should never be taken for granted. That day in the cafeteria when Bill asked all about your trip with your family last summer, what you saw, what routes you took, where you camped, you found yourself chattering away like a travel agent. Later, at home, you mused, "Bill Lacy sure has personality!" Come to think of it, Bill had not said or done anything extraordinary, except to show an interest in *you.* And that was enough. In all areas of life, skill in human relations is based upon a genuine interest in other people. That goes for a party, school, a business office, a club, or anything else. It pays, too, to be interested in everyone you meet, especially in those who are "different," from whom some fellows and girls shy off. *"Different"* people are likely to be *interesting* people; and the wider your range of acquaintances, the broader will be your own horizons.

Do we need to add that personality reflects *good manners?* You know that you like to see and be with a fellow or girl who is courteous without being too obvious about it. To know the accepted rules of good behavior will help you over some awkward moments and answer such questions as how to make introductions, how to order a meal in a restaurant, how to answer a written invitation, how to telephone an office, what to say after you have been introduced, and countless other puzzlers. It's all very simple, and there are rules that make it so. Some of these you will find in Chapter 8.

Closely allied to interest and skill development is growth in the art of *appreciation.* Does that sound a bit longhair? As a matter of fact, you are developing your powers of appreciation constantly; and if you are serious about improving your personality, you will never take any pleasant experience for granted, but will try to appreciate each one. This refers to simple, common things like a sunshiny day, a beautiful snowstorm, a good meal, a walk with your dog, a campfire, as well as things or circumstances somewhat less commonplace. You can recognize and appreciate equally well a good jazz band and a symphony orchestra; a rousing historical novel and a poem that says some things you feel inside you, but cannot express; a tiny flower garden and the Grand Canyon; the love of a little child and the applause of a large audience.

All these circumstances and things you can appreciate at the time, and better still, store them away in your memory to enrich your life and thus your personality. "First the better, then the best" in all areas of interest is a wise objective.

Without worrying or pushing too hard, gradually strengthen those points mentioned above where you feel weak. Gradually, week by week, month by month, you become more gracious, a better companion, a more interesting person; and a new personality will shine through.

5

Keeping Those Emotions in Hand

MOST OF THE WONDERFUL, THRILLING experiences we have, as well as our tough times, are the result of those strange, complicated feelings known as emotions. They make us happy or sad, "on top of the world" or "in the dumps," calm or upset, courageous or fearful.

We hear and read a great deal today about "emotionally disturbed" or "emotionally immature" people, and we infer from all we are told that emotional maturity is tremendously important. So what's it all about? Where does this maturity fit into our lives and our futures? Does it have anything to do with our moods and our upsets? If so, we had better do something about them.

First, let's understand the physical effects of our emotions. There are five basic emotions, and you have felt every one of them: anger, joy, love, grief, and fear. We have plenty of other feelings, too, that stem from or are forms of these five: anxiety comes from fear, irritation is a mild form of anger, sympathy is closely related to love, and so on. All our emotions start with stimuli, either from the outside or the inside, and they strongly influence our behavior and thus our personalities.

At an exciting basketball game you may be happy, fearful, or proud, your emotions changing from minute to minute during the game. These emotions come from stimuli *outside* yourself. They come from the game. But weeks later, you recall with pride and satisfaction the victory that the team won that night, or the fun you had at Joe and Sue's afterward. Then the stimulus comes from *within* you, from your memory brain centers.

When a stimulus comes your way, what happens? Those stimuli spark the nervous system to send messages to certain glands or organs of the body to order them to start work to cope with the situation. When we get angry, the adrenal glands, located at the top of the kidneys, pour hormones into the blood. When we are confronted with an emergency situation and must act quickly, as when Bill dived into the lake for his young sister who had fallen out of the boat, the liver releases sugar into the blood to supply the extra energy needed. Our breathing is stepped up too under strong emotional stimuli, and the blood flows faster to carry energy to our muscles. With our bodies responding to emotions in ways like these, is it any wonder that we sometimes become red with anger or ill from fright?

Now our pleasant emotions we can take care of quite nicely. Of course we sometimes get too excited or too happily emotional, but those brief periods aren't usually very serious. It's the unpleasant ones that trip us up. And we all receive plenty of outside stimuli for creating the unpleasant variety, life being what it is. We get angry, frightened, disappointed, or experience other unpleasant feelings rather frequently. But these need not always be destructive forces. Anger has given people the courage to tackle some great wrongs. Grief has driven sufferers to find new and deep experiences in helping others.

Back in 1866 a man in New York City became deeply angry as he watched horses being cruelly beaten and dogs and cats neglected or abused. The Society for the Prevention of Cruelty to Animals was the result. Most of us, when we become angry for a good reason, cannot organize societies; but there are other ways to turn our anger to good ends. Ted saw a young lad being bullied by a sixteen-year-old six-footer. His anger brought Ted's boxing skill into play to right the wrong. Jane became angry when she noticed shy, awkward Nancy being snubbed by her crowd, and she became Nancy's good friend.

There are times when emotions like fear can be constructive too—when fear is not a symptom of weakness but of wisdom. A world-renowned mountain climber says that one difference between an amateur climber and a professional is that the professional knows when an ascent is too hazardous to attempt and the amateur does not. Caution based on good judgment is not fear. Nor is recklessness a form of courage, or taking foolish dares, bravery. All these are the marks of the amateur.

Everyone who drives a car has been tempted at one time or another to "open her up" to see just what she can do. There's a resulting thrill, half fear and half daring. No doubt about that. But it's still kid stuff, because it is flirting with danger.

It isn't always possible to turn our unpleasant emotions to constructive uses, and we cannot avoid having them either. Everybody at one time or another is plagued by worry over small things, oversensitivity, regret for things he wishes he hadn't done, getting excited too easily, and losing his temper. These seem to head the list of the emotional problems of young people, based on studies made by the "experts." We cannot ignore these unpleasant emotions, but how we handle them is what counts for or against us. Take anger, for instance. Somebody does something that makes us angry, maybe justifiably so. Our first impulse is to strike back. Children usually do. They slap or kick or bite. But the ten or twelve years that have intervened since our childhood days have taught us a few things. We don't kick or bite; that would be too undignified! But we do lose control of our tempers maybe, slam doors, stamp out of the room, make cutting remarks, write unkind notes. These are really ways of "striking back" too, and if we resort to them, we haven't progressed so far beyond our childhood days as we thought we had.

Now all this sounds very fine, but it's not helpful. What can emotionally mature fellows and girls do when they become upset, justifiably or not? There are some constructive ways for handling all kinds of emotional upsets, ways that will keep your self-respect and the respect of others and make you a happier, stronger person, whom others will soon look to for both friendship and leadership.

Anger bothers all of us a lot, so let's think about that first. There are some unfailing rules for handling anger before it gets to the boiling point.

Rule One: Don't lose control of yourself. The minute you lose control of yourself, you have lost control of the situation, admitted defeat, and weakened yourself. The old adage to "count ten" is as smart as it is ancient.

Joe was the capable, energetic project-committee chairman of a school club. He liked to see things done efficiently and quickly. So Joe went ahead "on his own" without consulting his committee, made decisions, and spent money. The president of the club had no choice but to reprimand Joe, which he did as tactfully as he could. And was Joe mad! He "blew his top" and threatened to resign. "Some guys certainly have no appreciation!" he stormed to anyone who would listen. Thus Joe "fought back" and perhaps for the moment got some childish satisfaction from his behavior—like kicking a door that has jammed your finger. But Joe paid too big a price for revenge. He demonstrated that he could not take criticism or consider a situation calmly or evaluate himself objectively. Joe was never elected to an office in that group again, capable though he was. Even more serious, Joe was forming habits that would jeopardize his future; because unless we learn self-control in our teens, it's mighty hard to develop it later in life, when we have to exercise it or be defeated in things far more important than club elections.

But suppose the criticism of Joe had been unjust and uncalled for? What then? The first rule stands, and for the same reasons. If Joe, despite his hurt, could have remained calm and brought himself to say to the president, "Okay, Bob, but let's talk this over. I think there's something to be said on my side too," he would have in a flash won Bob's respect and gratitude, demonstrated to the whole group that he was levelheaded and reasonable, and added immeasurably to his personal stature. That's grown-up behavior, and it's the kind that brings you grown-up respect and consideration. If you deserve it, you get it.

Rule Two: When you become very angry, recall immediately how others have looked to you when they lost their tempers. Ridiculous? Funny? Frightening? Not a very attractive picture, whatever form it takes. Nobody is interested very much in your anger except *you,* so a display of temper accomplishes nothing except making your pals want to give you a wide berth until you cool off.

Rule Three: Put your angry energy to work. "Marie makes me so mad!" Betty stormed, as she dashed into the house and grabbed her tennis racket. "If I don't work off some steam, I'll pull her hair!" Sounds amusing, but Betty was smart. It's amazing how quickly anger cools down with a physical workout. Better hit a tennis ball than a friend, or take a brisk walk around the block than say things you will be sorry for later.

Rule Four: Face yourself squarely and fairly and decide whether you are to blame, at least in part. If you honestly decide that you are not, forget about it and avoid unreasonable or unfair people insofar as you can. If you are to blame, prove your bigness of spirit and apologize. You will lose nothing but some selfish vanity that you are better off without, and you will gain your own and everyone else's resepect and friendship.

Another crippling emotion is *fear,* and it's a common one too. Everybody is afraid of something. Some of our fears are justified and some are not, but in either case they can make us miserable and ineffective. Of course, sudden fear, the result of physical danger, cannot be helped. It has to be coped with as well as possible by keeping a level head. But the fears and anxieties that plague us for longer periods, we can really get to work on and conquer.

It is important, first, to recognize the fear for what it really is. Pulling it out into the open is the first step toward mastering it. Why are we afraid to go to the dentist? Because we are afraid we shall be physically hurt a bit, and we know that's childish. A few minutes' subjection to the dentist's drill is a small price to pay for sound and good-looking teeth. That kind of fear is not only immature but also very unintelligent, and to give in to it is pretty silly. We ought to be able to climb up over that particular fear rather easily, if we recognize it for what it is.

Some young students are afraid to recite in class, especially to make some kind of oral presentation in front of the class. What is your real fear, if this is one of your favorite brands? If you dig down deep enough, you may find that you are worrying about the impression you will make, your clothes, your appearance. So it is *yourself* you are worrying about and not your report or the people who will listen. Every successful speaker has learned to keep his mind on what he is saying and not on himself. That isn't always easy. It takes practice. But if you have something to say, get interested in your subject, prepare yourself thoroughly, and then try to transfer your interest to the group. If you are talking about the latest expedition to Antarctica, for example, keep your mind on those explorers and their surroundings and the thrilling time they are having. You want your audience to see it as you do. Then practice making your report at home, *aloud,* because no matter how well prepared you are, the sound of your own voice may startle you and throw you off. So give your report aloud to your mirror several times. Keep at it, and gradually you will not only overcome your fear, but add a valuable skill to your personal equiment.

If you dread an exam in school (as who doesn't?) or the test to get your driver's license, it is probably because you are not so well prepared as you should be. Admit the real cause of your fears and have a few more regular sessions with those books or get more instruction and practice with the car.

Are you afraid of social occasions, of meeting new people, of talking to new boys or girls? Is this because you feel awkward, ill at ease, strange? Read Chapter 3 again and Chapter 6, "It's a Date!" Some of your fears may be mentioned there. You may need to develop more poise, more conversational ease. Once again, if you keep your mind on the other person instead of on yourself, much of your fear will disappear.

You may have a purely physical fear, like fear of water or

thunderstorms or the dark. Perhaps when you were small, you were frightened in the water and you have never had the courage to dive. Or your fear may be of some person, a teacher whom you fear because you don't like the subject he or she teaches.

Whatever your fears, once you recognize them for what they are, the next step is to do something about them. Some ways of tackling them have been suggested above. Talk with the teacher about that subject you fear. Be frank and explain that you hope to do better. Then study a bit harder. In a social situation, remember that the other person may be afraid too. Begin by finding another shy person and making friends, by talking in a friendly way to younger children (this helps wonderfully in cultivating your conversational powers), by passing the time of day with older people whom you know—all the while thinking of them instead of yourself. If it's confidence you need, learn to do something well. Nothing builds confidence like success.

If you are afraid of a home situation, try helping along a bit more, keeping the rules laid down by Mother and Dad, and avoiding arguments and upsets. Look through Chapter 9 for hints on living successfully with the family.

We seem to have come up with two or three definite rules for handling fears and anxieties.

First: Face your fear honestly and recognize it for what it is. Don't excuse or hide or deny it, but decide what or whom you fear.

Second: Find out the cause of your fear. Is it physical? Is it the result of shyness? Is it the result of neglect on your own part, lack of experience, an immature attitude?

Third: Do something about it. Begin gradually, in easy stages, to tackle your fear.

Another crippling emotion is jealousy. The first time a baby was brought into your house and the family dog saw you petting it, he tried to get between you and the baby or maybe he showed his teeth. Perhaps your own small brother or sister showed a similar emotion. Animals and children are easy prey to this emotion we call jealousy. But jealousy knows no age limits. Young people and much older folk are quite commonly jealous, even though this is one of the most unattractive and vicious emotions one can entertain. Jealousy stems from fear and selfishness, and most of us are ashamed of our weakness, but we cannot keep it under cover. In one way or another we let it be known to all viewers that we are jealous, usually because somebody is getting more attention than we are.

Now as we have done in the case of other emotions that make us unhappy, let's drag this one out into the open and face it for what it is. We are jealous of people because we are afraid that we are inferior to them in some way. Sue is jealous of Beth's popularity at school because she believes, perhaps almost unconsciously, that Beth has social talents that are superior to hers. That psychological truth about jealousy was demonstrated recently at a country 4-H Club exhibit, where two fellows had poultry and cattle entries.

In spite of himself, Jack could not stifle some pretty sharp feelings of jealousy when his beautiful White Leghorns got only a passing nod from the judges and Ned's got a blue ribbon. Ned was rather heady about it too, which didn't help matters. Jack avoided Ned all day. Then came the cattle-judging, and Jack's Black Angus got first prize. Suddenly Jack was no longer jealous. He too had won success.

Rather than waste your energy, make yourself miserable, and lose the respect of your friends, who can always "see through" that childish behavior, it is smart to congratulate or co-operate with the one of whom you are jealous and then turn your attention to both your limitations and your talents. If a friend wins an election you wanted, get in there and work for him; at the same time cultivate your own favorite skill or hobby, for at this point you need to feel *success*. To do something for the one who, you are afraid, has surpassed you is a tough assignment, maybe, but only a really big person could meet it. Prove to yourself and others that you are such a big person, and miraculously your jealousy will disappear.

Even though you may control or overcome anger or jealousy, the disappointment remains. Perhaps you are not angry or jealous at all, but disappointed only. And that is bad enough. Disappointed that some cherished plan fell through, that a "date" did not materialize, that you got a poor grade in spite of conscientious study, that a friend let you down, that you have to abandon plans for college, that somebody else landed the summer job.

"Life is full of disappointments" is a cliché that doesn't make them any easier to accept. But there are ways that do make disappointments easier to handle.

Nancy's program was a complete flop, or so she believed. One participant didn't show up, the violin soloist broke his A string, and at the most impressive moment something blew a fuse and all the lights went out! The first thing Nancy did upon her arrival home after that harrowing ordeal was to fling herself down on her bed and burst into tears. Smart Nancy! For girls get emotional relief through a good cry (which is quite different from being a chronic crybaby), just as boys get it through a session with the punching bag.

The next step in this therapeutic treatment for disappointment may be to "talk it out." Betty telephoned a friend who shared her disappointment. They "griped" and grieved together until, before the end of the conversation, they had actually found something funny in the situation. A sense of humor always helps. In a few days, Betty was busy at something else. Find a physical outlet if you need it, talk it out or think it through, accept it, and then get busy at something else to compensate for the bad letdown you have experienced.

This is all fairly easy, if your disappointment does not affect the course of your life, thwart your ambitions, or hurt you deeply. Admittedly, such disappointments are harder to take. But before you give in to bitterness or hopelessness, remember some of those great people of the world who have triumphed over crushing disappointments. As a matter of fact, everyone who has accomplished anything in this world has had to do just that. Beethoven, after a long struggle supporting an alcoholic father and younger brothers and sisters, finally, at twenty-eight, seemed to be approaching success, only to discover that he was losing his hearing. What greater tragedy could come to a musician? But Beethoven did not stop composing, he did not lose faith in himself, he did not give up. He continued writing his immortal music, although some of his greatest he himself never heard, for he became totally deaf long before he died. Beethoven accepted his disappointment, his grief, his tragedy, and went on from there. And so can you in order to attain a greater success, deeper happiness, a more splendid achievement, than you had ever hoped for. Thousands and thousands of people have done it. For life takes away with one hand and gives with the other. That is a handy bit of philosophy to latch onto as you keep meeting and facing up to disappointments, large and small, important or trivial.

Some young people are up against a handicap in the form of a physical defect, extreme poverty, the race into which they were born. You may be one of these, and you may feel, understandably too, that these are frustrating blocks to your ambition, that you were licked before you started out on life's race through some of these circumstances over which you have little or no control. If this is true, you might reasonably have read all the above with the idea constantly in the back of your mind, "This sounds fine for average fellows and girls, but it isn't for me. I'm handicapped."

The obvious comment to make at this point would be to call attention to those many famous people who have been tremendously successful against all such odds. But these people were or are geniuses of one kind or another, and you probably are not. You may be sure, however, that thousands of unknown people with just such handicaps as yours, or worse, are living lives of usefulness, nobility, and happiness. How do they do it? How do they climb up over emotions of bitterness, disappointment, fear, and hopelessness?

The first suggestion, which comes from some of these people, is: you must start right where everybody else starts, with what you have been given, good and bad. You cannot often change other people, or even always your environment or circumstances. But you can take *yourself* in hand. That's the first and most difficult thing for all of us to do (it's so easy to take the other fellow in hand!) but it is half your battle. Look straight into that mirror without fear or shame or rebellion. Face and accept your handicap with what grace you can muster and go on from there. Don't use it as a refuge to hide behind or as an excuse, or even a reason, to abandon the blueprint for your life. You are of a minority race. You are crippled from an attack of polio. You are a poor student and cannot pull your grades up to passing. You have no home, or the home you do have is seriously disturbed.

These are not trifles. They are sometimes big and tragic situations. But you need not be licked by any one of them.

Second, do not waste your precious mental and emotional energy by futile questions or self-pity or bitterness. These attitudes only add to your problem and keep you so emotionally upset that soon you have a double handicap to cope with. Instead, take a deep breath and start some constructive program for your life. You can prepare blueprints commensurate with your abilities and circumstances. A young woman who had been permanently crippled in an automobile accident but who has done some really amazing things despite her misfortune said to a group of friends:

> For over a year after the accident I wept, rebelled, and asked myself and anybody else who would listen, "Why did this have to happen to *me?*" One day, how or why I shall never know, some grain of good sense popped into my consciousness and I took myself in hand. "You're going to be just this way for the next forty years or so. Tears and bitterness and self-pity won't change anything. Is this the way you want to spend your life?"

She did not need to carry her story further. What had happened when this brave girl stopped concentrating on her personal tragedy and started making plans for her future was quite obvious. The extra effort she was forced to put forth turned up abilities she never dreamed she possessed. One forgot she was crippled when watching her lead the youth group of which she was then president.

This girl's experience leads into a third suggestion. Look over your own equipment and circumstances. What can you do, or what can you learn to do? Secure, first of all, the soundest education or training you can get. If your physical activities are limited, or if you have a different type of handicap, related to circumstances which neither you nor time can change, train your mind or cultivate some skill you can handle. Should it be some form of art? Music? Work with children? A handicraft? Gardening? Mechanics? Cooking? Sewing? The point is, for your own sake, decide what you would like to do, what your natural interests are, what you are able to do, and then learn to do it *supremely well.* You need the feeling of success and achievement that such a skill will bring to you.

There are many sources of aid if you need it, either in the form of ideas or more practical help. Some of these are listed in the Source Books at the back of this book.

Finally, keep constantly in mind that many of the circumstances of your life will change. Science is constantly perfecting cures for disease and illness. Opportunities for young people of every race are growing at a rapid pace. Your own personal environment, if unhappy, is only temporary. In a few years you will be on your own. Meanwhile look yourself and your opportunities over and start building your life.

Carlyle once wrote something very wonderful about "the heroic that slumbers in every heart." Do not smother the hero in your own heart and soul. Refuse to surrender to circumstances, even as you admit their existence, but face life prayerfully, hopefully, and unafraid. Your gallantry will encourage others and bring big returns to your own life.

6

It's a Date!

Or is it? If you are just entering your teens, perhaps you are beginning to wonder how soon you will begin to date, when you will "fall in love," and whether or not the boys, if you are a girl, or the girls, if you are a boy, will find you attractive. That is a natural concern, but it is important that you keep one thing in mind, and it is this: if now, or later, you permit your desire to be popular with boys or with girls to get the upper hand or to take up too much of your thoughts, your overeagerness will ruin your natural personality and defeat the very purpose you have in mind. We have all seen girls and boys try to "show off" in some way to attract attention—to talk and laugh too loudly and at times when they have to force it, to be rude or coarse, or in some other way to "put on an act." Such behavior is not only unattractive, but also pretty obvious to everybody and rather pitiful.

If you are in your middle or late teens and date rarely or not at all, you may be getting worried. "Is there something wrong with me?" "What has Sally or Bill got that I haven't got?" "Won't I ever be married?"

These too are normal concerns, and you would be surprised

if you knew how many happily married people had the same worries in their teens or even later. So—early, middle, or late teens, as your age group may be—here are some helpful guide-posts on the royal road to romance. Some of them are "do's," and some are "don'ts."

First, remember the warning given just above. Don't let your wish to have dates spoil your personality.

Second, make yourself physically attractive. Boys like attractive girls, just as girls like attractive boys. To be attractive a girl does not have to be beautiful and a boy does not have to be handsome. Both should strive for clear complexions, good posture and carriage, becoming hairdos and clothes. Boys or girls are first attracted to you, as you are to them, by the appearance you make. Maybe you should turn back to earlier chapters and read them again at this point. Look yourself over in a mirror and make some notes.

Next to being physically attractive comes your personality, and this too we have discussed earlier. One important point is worth repeating: always be yourself and cultivate your own personality. Forced, unnatural behavior of any kind is fatal.

Now we come to a prescription for making new friends of both sexes, one that young people themselves say is the most helpful of all: acquire one or more social accomplishments. Learn to dance well. If a girl can master the new steps and be proficient at the old as well, she does not have to be a smooth talker to have partners, and dates will follow. And no boy need be shy about asking a girl to a dance if he is known as one of the best dancers hereabouts.

If athletic activities are more in your line, then make a real name for yourself on the tennis court, on the swimming team, or in some other sport where groups participate and where your skill will be a definite social asset. Have you a voice that is worth cultivating? You may never make the Metropolitan Opera Company, but a role in the high school operetta may, for you, bring bigger thrills. In brief, look over your interests and talents and get to work on them. Never say you have none worth bothering about. That just could not be true.

As a step up in the social scale, nothing is more rewarding than associating yourself with people with whom you have mutual interests. This is especially true of the shy fellow or girl. Dates and romance are usually the by-products of other activities. Young people who are interested in the same things become interested in each other. Many happy marriages take place between young people who possibly never dated at all in high school but who met and fell in love later in church, at a club, or on a trip, or when they were working together or became interested in some community project. So do not worry about those dates that never come. You can have fun, happiness, and high adventure doing well the things you like to do, and one day your true love will appear, probably at a moment when you are not looking!

While girls are waiting for dates to develop, it is sometimes a temptation to select one particular boy and start building, not only daydreams about him, but also rather definite plans for the future around him. Sometimes if a girl is dated once by a boy, she begins at once extending that date, in her mind, to a relationship with him that she has no right to expect. It is this attitude on the part of some girls that causes young men, particularly when they reach marriageable age, to be very wary about dating. Don't discourage a boy from approaching you for a date by this presuming attitude. Dates are fun in themselves. They are by no means always a prelude to "going steady."

And this brings up another question. Do boys like girls who chase them? Let's be honest and state at the outset that a few girls—and a very few—can telephone boys, single them out for their attention, and in other ways make proffers of special friendship without seeming to offend the boys or make them run in the other direction, but this is not the usual case. Most boys want to feel that they are the pursuers. They think this is their prerogative; as for that matter, it has always been throughout man's history. The sad fact is that if you feel that to get attention from a boy, you must pursue him, the chances are that it will get you nowhere with the boy. He may openly elude you or try to rebuff you without being rude, and that is embarrassing business for both. Every girl prefers to be sought out by a boy, but overconcern about dates prompts her to telephone him, to force herself on his attention, even to remember his birthday with gifts, and so on. This is wasted effort and ill-bred to boot.

There are other ways to let a boy know that you are about: casual and friendly conversation when the occasion arises naturally, invitations to affairs that are definitely girl-take-boy, sincere compliments on his accomplishments. Look for these opportunities for getting better acquainted with that boy who interests you, without sacrificing your self-respect and inviting his displeasure.

Another question that troubles some high-schoolers is, "How old should I be before I 'go steady'?"

Now the phrase "going steady" means different things in different communities. The going-steady period varies from two weeks in some localities to six months or longer in others. The older the couple, the longer the period, usually. The chief advantage of going steady seems to be that one is always assured of a date and of a partner at social affairs. For a boy, it is less expensive too than "playing the field," for there are many things a couple who are going together more or less regularly can do that do not cost anything, whereas a new date has to be escorted somewhere more formal—which usually involves an admission charge.

If going steady is kept on a "good pal" basis, it may work out satisfactorily for both concerned. But it usually cannot be, and if taken seriously by one or the other, somebody is likely to get hurt. Eventually, the boy or the girl tries to break up the relationship, and this is embarrassing.

Then, of course, going steady when you first begin to have dates limits your circle of boy or girl friends. You do not have the opportunity to make new friends or to find out what qualities in boys or girls you really prefer, because one person is taking up all your time. This means too that going steady limits the freedom and independence that most of you want.

Your age has a direct bearing upon whether or not you go steady. Many happy marriages take place shortly after a girl, at least, graduates from high school. But if either the girl or boy is headed for college or advanced training of some kind, the chances are the two will grow apart as new interests and new friends come into their lives. Then their situation will be less unhappy if the relationship has not been too "steady."

Even though you do not want to go steady, you may have run into some parental objection to your dating at all, if you are not yet sixteen, for example, or perhaps even older. Let's admit that Mother and Dad should have the final word about this. They are legally and morally responsible for you and probably have their good reasons for objecting to your dating seriously just now. Could your own behavior have anything to do with those reasons? Do you keep your word about getting home at a promised hour? Is your behavior always mature and responsible, or do you sulk or whine or even cry when things don't come your way? That kind of childish behavior, let's face it, doesn't encourage anybody to believe that one can take care of himself as an independent, intelligent young person should. Anyway, even if you are not permitted to have formal dates, there are plenty of opportunities for you to enjoy your friends, even a special friend, at school affairs, at church functions, in community activities. And you can organize parties of your own: at home, at the beach, a "cook-out," a foursome for skating with a buffet afterward. These affairs help a dateless boy or girl to have fun too, just as long as you do not try to "buy" dates or popularity with party-giving. If you want to have a party of any kind, have it for the sake of the good time you will give to others and yourself, and let that be your only motive. Then you will really enjoy yourself with no resulting disappointments.

This whole subject of dates and interest in the opposite sex is a fascinating one because it originates in that wonderful physical force that brings romance into our lives, makes us fall in love, create our own homes, and have children. Scientists would express this another way. They would say that sex is nature's way of guaranteeing that the human race and other living things reproduce themselves and thus perpetuate life.

But sex to human beings means many more things than physical reproduction. It makes work and play among boys and girls and men and women more fun, more interesting, and more worth while, because each sex has its own contributions to make to all of life's activities. We have in America, more commonly than in almost any other country, co-ed activities—clubs, sports, various types of societies, community projects, and all kinds of social and working contacts. The "experts" are agreed that comradeship in these situations leads to marriages that have a solid basis for happiness. Such comradeship often results in friends' "falling in love." And now you may be asking yourself, or someday you doubtless will be asking, "How can I know when I am really in love?"

"Love" is a fuzzy word. It means many different things when applied to that special boy or girl. It means first, of course, the physical attraction that he or she has for you. But it involves also unselfishness and generosity, understanding, patience, comradeship, and other mental and emotional qualities that are absolute "musts" if you are really in love and ready for marriage. You will probably be "in love" more than once before you marry. At least you will experience strong emotional feelings toward a certain boy or girl, which will make you believe you are in love. Then the circumstances of your life may change, and the first thing you know, you are beginning to have the same feelings about some other young man or girl. "Just what *is* this?" you will ask yourself. Well, you are in love both times, but to be sure you want to *marry* a particular person is something else again. When can you be sure about that?

Perhaps the first consideration is your age. Being in love when you are under eighteen, for example, is probably temporary, serious as it may seem at the time. Under certain conditions you could rather easily transfer your affections to someone else. But when you have finished your education—or at least high school, or college if you go farther than high school—and have found your vocational choice, then your tastes and interests are pretty well established. Then if you "fall in love," your romantic feelings are likely to be coupled with other things that make for a solid and happy marriage: similar interests, common backgrounds (there may be exceptions to this), dispositions that get along well, plus feelings of tenderness, generosity, respect, and loyalty.

If you are sure that you have all these attitudes toward your loved one, you are probably in love "for keeps" and ready for marriage. With such a foundation your marriage will be a three-way partnership between you, your husband or wife, and God.

Much of the joy and pleasure you will experience in both your dating and married life later on will depend upon how well informed you are about the physical aspects of sex and how wholesomely you regard your relations with boys and girls. The strictly physical facts of our wonderful reproductive capacities you have studied or will study in some of your school courses, usually in biology and physiology. These facts are easily learned and understood. You have a right and a duty to yourself to be fully informed about the physical aspects of sex. This information is easily obtained through the printed material available too. So get intelligent, accurate information, which will satisfy your desire for the truth and quell unhealthy curiosity. Young people are easily led into trouble just through curiosity. When you are well informed, you will be prepared to face your own physical and emotional problems and work on them intelligently, without fear or shame.

What is not so simple are the questions and problems that sex raises with you socially and in other daily situations. One of these is likely to be: "Is it wrong to indulge in petting or love-making with my date? If so, how can I avoid it? The fellows and girls seem to expect it."

Well, let's answer that one straight. Yes, promiscuous petting, with somebody you do not intend to marry, is wrong, and for several very good reasons.

First, petting is dangerous. Most young people know this, which is perhaps one reason they indulge in it; they like to flirt with danger, to see how far they can go and get away with it. Sexual intercourse between husband and wife who respect and love each other is often preceded by love play in the form of caresses and fondling. This demonstration of love and understanding of each other's needs increases sexual desire, as it was meant to do, and that sexual desire is then satisfied by sexual union. Excessive petting indulged in merely for a thrill easily results in a girl's loss of chastity, an illegitimate child, a boy's loss of respect for both the girl and himself, perhaps loathing on the part of both (for the first sexual union is usually accompanied by pain on the part of the girl), and an intimate experience which both would like to be able to forget later but never can. This is, of course, assuming that the boy and girl involved are normal, wholesome young people who do not make a practice of passing themselves around like a soiled bill of exchange.

Second, petting is wrong because it is cheating on one's partner, no matter how much he or she may invite it. A girl who permits a boy to fondle her (even though he may initiate it) arouses sexual desires in him which she probably has no intention of satisfying. This is not fair. And a boy who demands petting from a girl is probably asking her to lower her standards and to give him privileges which he hopes the girl he marries will not have given to anyone before him. This is cheating of the lowest kind.

Third, heavy petting soon loses its thrill and becomes a bore and a repulsion. And this emotional state is arrived at very soon, especially with girls, whose sexual desires may not be so strong as a boy's.

Even more important, during a true courtship the anticipation of marriage and complete union with one's husband or wife is considerably dampened, if not spoiled altogether, if heavy petting or sexual intercourse has already been experienced. The great joy that accompanies final union with the person one loves has been seriously marred with these premarital experiences.

The best way to avoid petting is to avoid the situations that lead to it, at least insofar as you can. Parked cars and lonely rendezvous are open invitations to petting. Foursomes and larger parties, sports, movies, and other forms of fun offer many pleasures less intimate. There are times, however, when boys and girls like to be alone with their dates. On such occasions it pays to remember two things. First, if a girl invites or initiates petting, she is admitting to her date that she lacks other attractions and hopes to be able to buy his attention through arousing his sexual desires. That kind of girl isn't worth your time. Second, if the girl does not want to pet, but the boy seems so inclined, she can turn his first attempts off lightly and with good nature. If the boy is the kind you can like and respect, that will probably do the trick. If he insists, then you must decide whether or not he is dating you only for one purpose. If so, you have nothing to gain by his cheap attentions and everything to lose.

You will be interested in the actual statements, uncensored, of some young people on this subject of petting. You may find expressed in some of these statements a code or standard which you would like to follow.

"I went with a boy for over a year, and we liked each other

a lot. But am I glad I can still look him in the face without remembering any hot party!"

"I had intercourse with a boy once and afterward I was sick with fright, and so was he. I learned a lesson the hard way."

"If you're attractive and lots of fun, you don't have to pet to be popular with the boys."

"Some of the fellows think girls expect you to kiss them, and even more. If they wouldn't ask for it, lots of guys would like them better."

"Heavy petting is phoney. It makes you nervous and you get awfully sick of it."

"I'm engaged now and both of us are awfully glad we have our complete marriage to look forward to, without remembering experiences that would spoil everything now."

Falling in love and getting married is a wonderful business—too wonderful to run the risk of spoiling. Remember always that true love-making is not a matter of the physical body alone. It unites the mind and spirit and results in the all-round well-being of the two who love each other. Remember too that sex is only one interesting feature of a highly interesting world.

There is something pretty wonderful about an attractive fellow who helps his date be her best, always, and that's true of the girl's part, too. Yes, boys, there are girls who "ask for it," who chase you, who encourage shoddy behavior. And, girls, there are plenty of boys who will not date a girl unless she pets or drinks or otherwise lowers her standards (although some of them talk this way without honestly meaning it; if they like a girl, they will come back).

Boys can handle this situation easily; they can simply give silly girls a wide berth and date those with whom they can have wholesome good times. But girls have a more difficult time of it. There may be relatively few boys in a community or school to date. And it often seems that the "easy" girls get the attention. So they sit at home or have an all-girl social life. Even so, dates are not worth selling yourself short for. Look about you, girls, and you will see that most girls marry, and not because they were easy marks for second-rate fellows, but because some fine boy fell in love with their charm, their attractive appearance, their capacity for friendship, or some other quality that drew the two together. So we repeat earlier advice to both fellows and girls. Instead of worrying about being dateless, make yourself into the kind of person you want to be, and the dates will come along—dates that you don't have to buy with intimacies and coarseness and behavior that leaves a bad taste in your mouth and shame in your secret heart.

Girls, are the boys in your school "just kids?" If not, yours is the lucky exception, for across the nation high-school girls complain of the fact that the boys are not grown up. They "horse around" on dates, never want to talk about anything interesting, do not have good manners, and lack all the other characteristics of young men. You fellows who are reading this, be warned that you had better get "hep" to yourselves. The girl of your dreams may be driven to dating a fellow home from college or somebody who already has a job or even some old guy of thirty! And girls, although it is flattering to be dated by a fellow some years older than you, it would be wise to remember that he is probably not taking you too seriously. You cannot show an intelligent interest in his work or other phases of his life, and he is definitely not interested in high school and your favorite recordings, except for the occasion of your date. He is likely to treat you like a young sister, or be amused—not unkindly—by your youth. You can be almost sure that he is not taking you seriously. That is not very flattering to you, or very gratifying. Better be patient with the boys your own age, or just a few years older, who one day will seem suddenly to have grown up overnight. It is the fate of girls and women to feel at times older than the young men they date or even marry. Men, as one girl expressed it, are "grown-up little boys." But in many situations, girls also are—to the boys they date—childish, unreasonable, and so illogical! And let's admit, girls, that young as some boys behave, there are many situations that they are more than well equipped to handle: when you need a strong muscle, for example; or the radio fixed; or a tire changed; or just some good, solid masculine sympathy! In the end, things have a way of evening up, and for all-round satisfaction and fun, three or four years is about the widest gap desirable between the ages of a girl and her date.

Fascinating and important as romantic love is, like most of the finest things in the world, it is a delicate mechanism: fun—yes; something to be desired and anticipated—yes; but not to be abused or given all our attention. A wide, wide world of adventure and achievement lies ahead of you in many areas—education, your chosen vocation, travel to far places—to mention only a few. For life, as well as love, is a many-splendored thing.

7

Meeting Outside Pressures

YOU FELLOWS AND GIRLS IN YOUR teens are walking across a bridge—a long, wonderful span that leads from childhood to adulthood. As you walk across this bridge, you are meeting other groups of people. Some of them are making the crossing, just as you are, because they too are in their teens. Others seem to be accompanying you because they are helping to direct your way—your parents, teachers, adult friends.

These two groups of people are constantly bringing pressures upon you. Some of these you welcome and like; others you resent and even rebel against at times. You are likely to welcome the pressures that come from your own friends, pals of your age group, because you need to feel that you belong with that group. The pressures, on the other hand, that come from your parents and older friends, you may not always like because you want to be independent of authority and to make your own choices and decisions. Do you ever feel caught between two feelings, between wanting very much to grow up and be independent and at the same time wanting to remain a teen-ager, without having to face the decisions that adulthood brings?

In a later chapter we shall think about getting along with

the family, parents in particular, without unnecessary friction. Just now, let's concentrate on the other group, pals and acquaintances of your own age. To want to conform with your age group in many areas of your life is normal and desirable. It isn't absolutely necessary that you do so, but it's probably healthy that you want to wear the same styles that other high-schoolers in your community are wearing, to enjoy the same music, to have similar hobbies and social patterns. Some of these your parents and teachers may think are pretty weird, but they are all symptoms of the growing-up process and are usually your personal affair. It is a more serious type of conformity that causes trouble—when you value the opinion of the gang so highly that you are pressured into doing something you don't really want to do or into being the kind of fellow or girl you don't really want to be.

Nancy could have made good marks in school and sailed into the college of her choice on a scholarship. But to be known as a "brain" was to be avoided at all costs in her school, so she was pressured by public opinion into doing a lot less than her best. But Nancy never did feel right about it. For one thing, she knew she was letting Mother and Dad down pretty badly. They did not ask that she be a "longhair," but only that she make the best of herself.

Bill lived in a fine community and had many privileges. These included summer camp and a fair weekly allowance for spending money. It was not poverty and lack of care that sent Bill into a gang when he was fourteen. It was his natural wish to "belong." The gang included all types of boys—some from substandard areas of the city and some from wealthy families. The gang was not tough at the start, but a couple of leaders took over and the tough element grew. First pranks, then petty thievery, then drinking and lawlessness that finally got Bill into a serious jam.

Bill told his father that he was "chickened" into it. What he meant was that he could not resist pressures from his pals. In her situation, Nancy was likewise chickened into being something far less than her best.

Sometimes the pressures we meet have less serious consequences, but they are equally crippling. Girls are often pressured into gossip by companions who like to talk about people. Boys are pressured into timidity and cowardice when they permit somebody else to take the blame because nobody in the gang will come forward and confess his own responsibility. Some young people are pressured into pretending to enjoy rock-and-roll, when they really prefer the best in music.

What to do about this is probably the toughest assignment you have as a teen-ager.

There seem to be two attitudes you can take. The first is simple but not easy, and that is to take a firm stand and do what you think is right or refuse to do what you think is wrong, regardless of what anybody else thinks or says or does. You have a perfect right to say to yourself, "This is *my* life I am building. These are *my* habits and I alone have got to live with them, to fight them, or to let them control me. This is *my* reputation and nobody else's. This is *my* money to waste or spend wisely or have good fun with. What's ahead of me is *my future.*"

As we said, that isn't always easy, although it may work out to be a lot easier than you think, especially because you will probably influence some others, not quite so firm as yourself, to go along with you. They just need some encouragement and some companionship in the struggle! And never forget that there are always friends and pals to be had, even in your school and community, who won't insist on trying to live your life for you, to bring pressures to bear upon you, to chicken you into lowering your standards. They may not be the noisy, conspicuous fellows and girls, but they may prove to be very worth while, once you get acquainted with them.

The second attitude is a challenge too and has a direct bearing upon some things we have said about personality-building. Let's look at it this way. Nobody would ever expect a popular football player, for example, to be chickened into breaking training. Why? Because he has reached the place where he can set his own standards, whether he is in training or not. A socially successful girl who got the lead in the senior class play cannot be chickened into anything because she too has "arrived." So what are we really saying? Simply this, that you and every teen-ager can be the kind of friendly, respected, and popular person that sets his or her own standards and so is practically immune to pressures of the wrong sort. "But I can't make the football team!" "I have no dramatic talent!" Maybe not, but you can do other things and make your place. You can make a name for yourself in your own line of interests, and, along with your demonstrations of true friendship, head the parade instead of making up the mob that trails along behind. Even a poor little "dead-end" kid knows that if he can develop such physical power and skill that he can lick the other kids, he is in command and nobody can chicken him into anything! Borrow a page from his book on a higher level of life as you find it in your own situation, and begin to live as you really want to live.

Remember always that when you permit yourself to be chickened *into* something, you are at the same time permitting yourself to be chickened *out of* something else, of almost always the better thing. Don't let yourself be so pushed around.

Although Bill and Nancy did not realize it at the time, when they followed the gang and submitted to undesirable pressures from outside, what they were really doing was substituting for one kind of authority (the adult kind that they thought they didn't want) just another brand of authority, one that turned out to be much less desirable.

If you are attending a high school of almost any size and in almost any area of our country, the chances are you are being subjected to another form of pressure arising from the presence of sororities and fraternities or some other form of secret society in your school.

There are three points of view about this disturbing situation in American high schools. First, there is the point of view of you young people, whether you are among the "ins" or the "outs" of these societies. There is the view of your parents, who may be for or against them. And there is the view of the school authorities, who generally oppose such societies but who are frequently caught tight in the middle of the controversy.

If there are selective societies in your school, whether you belong to one or not, you do not need to have their demerits spelled out. You know what these are. Depending somewhat upon the local situation, these societies may be small and not too influential or they may be, at the other extreme, very powerful, snobbish, undemocratic, and even highly immoral. In some communities the law has had to step in when members of sororities and fraternities have allowed themselves to be pressured into petty crime or immoral behavior.

Strangely enough, this youth problem is one on which some parents take a stand that seems by many to be opposite to the

Christian, democratic position. Some parents are unalterably opposed to high school sororities and fraternities. Other parents, while opposed in theory, want their children to belong to them if they exist. "Life is undemocratic anyway," they argue. "My children will always be subject to approval or disapproval by society. I want them to learn to be accepted by the community." Other parents are afraid that if they speak out against these societies, they will embarrass their sons and daughters or be accused of having a "sour grapes" attitude.

You are the young people around whom this controversy swirls. Let's consider first the situation of the fellow or girl who has been passed by when the pledging season is on. If this has been your recent experience, you may feel left out, rejected, and worried for fear there is something seriously wrong with your personality. This feeling of rejection has been so serious that there are cases on record of girls attempting suicide because they did not make sororities in their high schools.

Now it is easy for an adult, far removed from the immediate problem, to point out that to be blackballed means nothing in terms of one's success, either socially or in any other area of later life. Teen-agers in high school lack judgment, are superficial in their appraisals, have silly prejudices, and so on. All that is true, but it is cold comfort to the rejectee. Or it is easy to point out that many great and successful and highly popular people were not in the "swing" of things in their youth. It is easy to advise that a young person rise above snubs and keep his eye on the higher objective of what he wants to be later in life. Young people have done just that, but it is never easy, when one is emotionally involved in a situation that exists right here and now.

What practical, sympathetic advice can be given, then? First of all, you must make up your mind that it will be up to you and no one else to handle this situation. You will have to ignore it insofar as you can and try to put disappointment and humiliation out of your mind. And the best way to accomplish this is to turn your attention, as was suggested in an earlier chapter, to some talent, skill, or ability that you can develop and thus bring satisfaction to yourself and attract the attention of others. Now this is not a purely selfish motive or program by any means, for in so doing you will be improving yourself, making the most of what God has given you, and preparing to help others in some capacity. Too many young people, confronted with some cruel disappointment, collapse into a state of bitterness, or fright, or crybaby defeatism. Do not permit any group in your school or community to classify you. Beat them at their own game and classify yourself as a talented, able, and at the same time friendly person to watch. You're going places!

Two sisters, in a community in which I once lived, entered high school from a depressed section of the city. They were poor, moneywise, and almost unknown except in the small group who had come from the same junior high school. Certainly they were not sorority "material." But those two sisters had been playing tennis for a few months because they loved to play and it did not cost anything to practice on the community courts. In a year's time they began to be heard from as "good" on the tennis court. In two years' time they entered the state junior matches. They had not learned to play tennis in order to "make" a sorority, and that is important. They had learned because they loved playing and were challenged by it. Sororities were "out" and they knew it; they could not afford them. Needless to say, when they became famous, the bids came in, and then sororities had become very unimportant to them.

Another girl of my acquaintance, who was almost painfully shy, learned the art of theatrical make-up and through this skill became not only much in demand, but also respected for her art, and of course she overcame her shyness. No matter what your situation or personality or—you may think—lack of accomplishments, there is something you can do to make yourself not only sought after, but also the fine person you were intended to be. You may find this difficult to believe, but you will, by cultivating some interest, suddenly discover that fraternities and sororities are not so important as they once seemed to be. But remember, if your motive in taking yourself in hand is only to become socially popular, you will probably fail at whatever you try to do. You will become uninterested or discouraged, because your basic objective is too superficial. On the other hand, if your motive is to improve yourself and to develop some worth-while skill, you will not only accomplish this, but also gain friendships among worth-while young people whose interests are like your own.

Now for the other side of the fence—to the "ins." Naturally you were flattered when you were "tapped," although perhaps in theory you do not believe in exclusive societies. They are smug and selfish. They demand so much time that they seriously affect your studies. Perhaps they have been banned by the authorities and so have gone "underground." Then the cases cited seem to prove they are particularly dangerous in their threats to high moral standards. What is your attitude to be?

Some time ago *Time* magazine wrote up the story of a girl in a Southern high school who belonged to a sorority and got so "fed up" with what went on that she started a one-girl crusade to abolish secret societies in the high school. This was news indeed, and *Time* magazine sent a reporter to get the story.

The girl crusader went first to the Parent-Teacher Association, where she found both approval and strong opposition. Eventually, through her efforts and those of others who shared her conviction but needed somebody to start the ball rolling, several very important reforms were introduced in the Greek letter groups, even though they did not disband. Blackballing was abolished; a C-average grade was required of pledgees; closing hours were made earlier; adult advisers were appointed. Parents who belonged to the P.T.A.'s connected with the elementary schools and whose children were to enter high school in a few years, voted to abolish Greek letter societies. This parental action carried a lot of weight—for many school authorities who have wanted to ban secret societies have been blocked by parents who wished their children to join them.

A one-man crusade may not be your dish, and probably is not; but you can work hard to make your organization more democratic, to raise its standards, to see to it that judgments are not superficial or snobbish, and most important of all, to reach out beyond your society and include other young people in your circle of friends. Don't be chickened into being a snob; like everything else, this gets to be a habit, and it is a mighty bad one. Don't allow yourself to be pressured into a rigid social pattern, even though you belong to a secret society which is based on false standards and which narrows your own horizon and shuts out interesting and worth-while friends.

Just anybody can be a feeble yes man. But it takes conviction and courage to tackle a wrong or to refuse to be pressured into a conformity you do not really like, and that's the thrill and challenge of life.

8

How's Your Etiquette?

GOOD MANNERS AND SOCIAL POISE are very important to you right now, for they are the best kind of treatment for self-consciousness and shyness. Knowing the rules of "smooth" behavior adds to your dating techniques and improves other school and community relationships too. Later, when you have entered college or found your place in the world of work, good manners will identify you to new associates as one who is well bred and self-assured and therefore likely to be a success at whatever you tackle.

Speaking in general, rules of etiquette may be divided into two groups: first, those that are based on kindness and consideration of others. These are by far the more important. They come almost naturally to some fellows and girls, whom we describe as "gentlemen and ladies at heart," whether or not they happen to know all the small rules that are followed in our modern social life. The second group of rules are simply customs that have, for one reason or another, come into general use by well-mannered people. Some of these have been handed down for many years, perhaps since the medieval age of chivalry. Others are more recent and have been accepted as standard custom for our particular time. These rules may change, as fashions change, from one generation to the next. What was considered polite a hundred years ago, like sipping tea from the saucer, is not done today.

But you want to be familiar with both kinds in order to fit into any social situation with ease and self-confidence. It is the *situation* that we meet first. Then come these questions of proper behavior. What should I do now? What is the proper thing to say? Is this the right way? And so on. So let's consider rules of etiquette and courtesy in the situation category.

Dating Manners

For the girl:

1. When a boy asks you for a date and you want to accept it, do so graciously. Remember, it may have taken some courage for him to approach you, so help him out by being natural. Don't pretend to be disinterested and don't be "gushy." "Yes, thank you, Bob, that would be fun. What time do you want to call by?"

If you cannot or do not want to accept his invitation, don't be unkind or rude, and don't hesitate and stall. Say frankly, "I'm sorry, Bob, but I can't make it that night." Or, "Thanks for asking me, Bob, but I have other plans for that day."

2. It is still the custom—and most girls prefer it that way—for the boy to take the initiative in dating, unless the occasion is an affair run by the girls to which each is expected to invite a boy. It is a big mistake for girls to telephone boys and practically ask for dates; or to hang around boys, waiting to be dated; or to resort to other schemes which are only too, too obvious. Most boys resent being pursued by girls. They like to feel that they are the pursuers. There are plenty of ways for a girl to

show that she is friendly, enjoys a boy's company, and would be good fun on a date.

3. Be ready when your date calls and be dressed appropriately for the occasion.

4. If he is a new date, not acquainted with your parents, introduce him to them. This can be brief. No need to make him uncomfortable with a long, drawn-out session. Your introduction will be simple. "Mother and Dad, this is Tom Bayley. Tom, these are my family!" (Mention your parents first in your introduction; the younger person is always introduced to the older.)

5. If this is a formal date and he has brought you flowers, thank him graciously (here again, don't embarrass him by overdoing it) and pin them on immediately. "Thank you, Bob. Isn't the color lovely with my dress?"

6. If this is just an evening to be spent wherever you like, he should ask you what you would like to do. Then make a definite suggestion and ask if he would enjoy it too. And keep in mind the probable state of his finances, but don't mention them! You couldn't make a more serious blunder than that.

7. If this is a new date, don't worry about what you will talk about or whether you can keep up a conversation. Remember, he is just as anxious to have a good time and to make a good impression as you are, so help him relax by relaxing yourself. Think about what your date is interested in, about school and community events, and start from there.

"The funniest thing happened in chemistry lab today."

"Is Jim going to be able to play in the game Saturday?"

"Have you seen the new history teacher? I hear he's pretty keen."

"We saw the Academy Award picture at the Bijou last Saturday."

If your date is on the quiet side, try to draw him out and be a good listener. Above all, don't force yourself to talk or laugh too loudly and too much. Remember, personality is not noisy. Be friendly, jolly, and interested in what he says and does, and you will have a successful date.

8. Whatever you are doing or wherever you are, don't fuss nervously with your dress or hair. The time for fussing is at home in front of the mirror. To comb one's hair in public, except possibly at the beach after a swim, is considered inexcusable by girls who really know their way about. Your date wants to see you looking nice. He doesn't want to see how you manage it.

9. When you reach home, thank him simply and sincerely. "It was swell, Bob, thanks so much." Don't linger long on the porch. Bob cannot courteously leave until you do, so don't make it necessary for him to explain to his parents, "Well, I didn't keep her out late. She talked and talked on the porch, so what could *I* do?"

10. Even though you hope very much that he will call you again, don't suggest it. Here again, he wants to take the initiative, and if he wants another date, he will ask for it. And that will be so much more flattering than if you hinted for it!

For the boy:

1. When you ask for a date, be definite about it. If you are new at this and feel shy about approaching that girl you have had your eye on, it will be a lot easier for you if you have something definite to suggest. Beating about the bush is always more

embarrassing than being direct. "I hear the picture at the Strand this week is tops. Would you like to go Friday night?"

2. If you are dating for the first time, don't try to date a girl who has been dating longer than you and steps out often. You run the risk of being turned down, which will make you still shyer. Anyway, you will probably have a better time with a girl who is a bit on the shy side herself. That will give you more confidence.

3. Arrive on time and go up to the door and ring the bell. Don't whistle from the sidewalk or blow your car horn. This is not "smart," as some fellows like to believe. It is ill-mannered and shows that you haven't been around. Never ask a girl to meet you anywhere either, unless under most extraordinary circumstances when such an arrangement is more convenient for her too, or when a group is involved.

4. Be dressed properly, as you expect her to be, and take flowers to your date if this is the custom. The florist will tell you what kind of corsage would be appropriate.

5. If you have not met her parents, greet them politely. Some parents are easier to meet than others, but regardless of their attitude, try to be at ease. Respond to the introduction by saying, "How do you do," not "Pleased to meet'ya." Don't talk too much, but to break the ice (if they don't) comment on the weather or where you are going. Don't sit down until they ask you to, and when either your date or her mother enters the room or gets up from her chair, you rise too. Don't hold it against your girl if her mother or father warns you to be home early. Remember, your parents often treat you like a little boy.

6. If you travel by bus, assist your girl up the step. You follow and pay the fares. If you have your car, open the door for her and close it after her, then come around the rear of the car

to your own seat. She'll be thrilled to see that you are a grown-up gentleman and not a callow youngster.

7. At a party she enters first, you both greet your hosts, and then you separate, if it is a home party, to take care of your wraps. Be sure you are on hand when she reappears, to escort her to the other guests.

Throughout the evening, you will be attendant upon your date. You will introduce her to others as necessary, accompany her for refreshments or bring refreshments to her, be her first partner for games and for the first dance, and see to it, if she is a stranger, that she is not left alone.

8. Be a good sport and get her home on time. That will help her out and give you a high rating with her parents.

At the Theater

1. The young man buys the tickets and hands them to the doorman or usher.

2. The girl precedes her date and follows the usher down the aisle to seats.

If at a movie and there happens to be no usher, the boy may take his date's arm and together they find seats.

3. Excuse yourself if you must ask somebody to rise or if you have to pass in front of him to get to your seats.

4. The boy helps his date take her coat off, and both remember the people behind them and settle in their seats quietly and quickly.

5. When leaving the theater, the boy always lets the girl precede him up the aisle.

In a Restaurant

1. In a restaurant or dining room the young man checks his coat while the girl waits, then the girl follows the head waiter

or the waitress to the table. The young man tells the head waiter how many seats they need. The head waiter will usually draw out a chair for the girl. If he does not, the boy should. This bit of gallantry girls appreciate. Simply draw her chair out far enough for her to sit and then push it in as she adjusts it to the table. Before he takes his own seat, he will help her place her wrap over the back of the chair, if she has not given it to him to be checked.

2. The boy hands the girl the menu. The girl gives her order to her escort, who gives both orders to the waiter or waitress.

It is not courteous or kind to keep a waiter standing too long while you decide upon your order. Wasting a waiter's time directly affects his income.

If you do not know what some items on the menu are, it is quite all right to ask the waiter to explain them.

Girls, if your date seems to be unsure of ordering procedure, relieve his embarrassment by giving your order to the waiter yourself. Some social customs are better broken than followed so slavishly as to create awkward situations.

Printed menus can be formidable affairs with their long lists of dishes, some with unpronounceable names. But don't let the menu throw you! Somewhere, probably smack in the center of those printed lists, you will find one headed "Table d'hôte." Translated into English this means "table of the landlord," but to you it means that the dishes listed there are complete meals, from "soup to nuts," at a fixed price. So instead of puzzling over unfamiliar names and possibly the highest prices, select a main course from the Table d'hôte list. Then order the appetizer (hors d'oeuvres) at the top of the menu (usually fruit juice or soup, sometimes both), then the main dish, your choice of vegetables if a choice is indicated, and indicate whether you prefer a beverage with your main meal or later with dessert. If the waiter does not ask for your dessert order, he will take it after you have finished the main course. Simple, isn't it?

You will see another list on the menu, headed "Entrees." This means that the courses under that heading are main courses only, and that you order separately and pay extra for appetizer, desert, and sometimes for beverage.

There are variations of these general menu plans, and if you are interested, you will have to study the menu to see just what is offered. Better not waste the waiter's time, however, or your escort's money if you are being dated, by "shopping around." Stick to the Table d'hôte for everybody's convenience.

When the waiter has brought your meal, or at least the first course, unfold your napkin and lay it across your lap. At the end of the meal, do not refold the napkin, but place it unfolded at the side of your plate.

3. All these rules apply to restaurants and dining rooms. When boys and girls drop into the drugstore for a coke, the girl does her own ordering. If it is a casual, spur-of-the moment snack, Dutch treat is often the rule too. Here courtesy is, as always, the smart way, but formality would be out of place.

4. Do not handle the silver or dishes while waiting to be served.

5. It is permissible to eat a roll or piece of bread while you are waiting, if these are already on the table.

6. If you need the waiter's attention during the meal, the young man beckons or waits until he is near enough to speak to him quietly.

7. Do not "sample" each other's food or "swap" helpings.

8. If anyone, boy or girl, man or woman, approaches your

table to speak to either of you, the young man rises. If one is unknown to another, make the introduction at once.

9. Always leave your spoon in the saucer, when not in use. And use your tea or coffee spoon only once, to test the temperature of your beverage. Do not sip from it. If no plate is served with iced drinks, leave the spoon in the glass, not on the table. When you have finished the main course, place the knife and fork across the plate. Never stack your dishes or set them to the side. It is the waiter's job to clear the table.

10. A girl will never embarrass her escort or make herself conspicuous by complaining about the food or the service. If either is bad enough to warrant it, the young man may explain quietly to the waiter. He may ask that the food be returned to the kitchen if anything is seriously wrong.

Whether you are in a restaurant or are being entertained at somebody's home, never begin to eat until all have been served.

If you are not sure about what silver to use, remember that the silver is placed at your place in the order of its use, beginning from the outside and working in toward your plate. For example, the soup spoon, if soup is the first course, will be at the outside right of your plate, and the first fork you will use will be at the outside left. Very few occasions are so formal that a puzzling variety of silver is called for, but you can always "bone up" ahead on such points with the help of that etiquette book you have borrowed.

When the meal is over, if the restaurant or dining room is a busy one, do not linger and so prevent your waiter or waitress from getting more customers.

The young man picks up the check and pays either the waiter (in which case the waiter will probably leave the check on a small plate or platter on the table) or the cashier on the way out.

The amount of the tip in most places is about twenty per cent of the total check.

The young man gets up from the table just as soon as his companion is ready, pulls her chair a short distance away from the table as she rises, helps her on with her wraps, and stands aside while she precedes him to the door, where she waits while he pays the check and gets his wraps.

With experience, customs and rules will come easily. Meantime it is more important that you be relaxed and at ease in formal places than that you know all the proper things to do. Don't be so worried about doing the right thing every minute that you are stiff and self-conscious. Behave quietly, be considerate, follow the fundamental rules of courtesy that you already know, and other things will gradually take care of themselves.

As a House Guest

If you put yourself in the place of your host or hostess and try to be the kind of guest you yourself would enjoy having around, you will probably be a "whale" of a success as "company."

You are probably the guest of the young people in the family, so the basic rule is to adapt yourself to the household routine as naturally and with as little trouble to the adults as possible.

1. Help with the household "chores," which means making your bed, wiping the dishes; or if at a camp or summer cottage, giving a hand with whatever you see needs to be done.

2. It means also that you neither keep the family awake by

talking after "lights out" or by getting in too late and then oversleeping and upsetting the breakfast schedule.

3. It is a pleasant gesture to bring your hostess some small gift, like candy or flowers, or to send it to her after you get home. This is not necessary, however. If you are a companionable, well-bred guest, you will have shown your hostess how much you have appreciated her invitation, and she will be more than repaid.

4. A bread-and-butter note is a "must," however, if you have spent a night or longer as a guest. Your note need not be long, but simply a sincere thank-you with possibly a mention of any special event or circumstance that you enjoyed.

Introductions

Making and acknowledging introductions can raise perplexing questions. First, how do you make introductions? The proper formal way is to say:

1. "Mrs. Blake, may I present my roommate, Sally Adams? Sally, this is our neighbor, Mrs. Blake."

Always address the older person first, because you are introducing the younger to the older.

Less formal, but still proper is:

2. "Mother, this is Bill Sykes, who has just come to our school."

3. If you are introducing two of your friends of your age, you say, "Jim, this is Peter Taylor from Dayton; he is visiting us."

4. Or if you introduce a boy to a girl, address the girl first, "Jean, this is my cousin, Jim Lake. Jim, Jean and I have been friends for a long time."

5. Always introduce a person of distinction by giving his name first: Major Gray, may I introduce Sergeant Thomas?

The general rule is: The person to whom you wish to show deference is always mentioned first.

Introductions to older people are acknowledged by saying simply, "How do you do, Mrs. or Mr. So-and-so." The older person should pick up the conversation from there.

It is customary for young people, especially when they meet informally, to respond simply by saying, "Hello, Bob." "Hello, Jean." "Hi, Bill."

What about shaking hands after an introduction? Young men and older men always shake hands when introduced. But the younger man waits for the older to take the initiative and extend his hand first.

Both fellows and girls shake hands if the person to whom they are introduced extends his hand. This is a gesture of good will.

Girls do not usually shake hands with young men when they are introduced; and they wait and follow the lead of the older person, man or woman, to whom they have been introduced.

When you are the host or hostess, always shake hands with your guests when they arrive and when they depart.

Young people *always* rise from their seats when introduced to or addressed by an older person. And of course young men *always* rise when they are introduced to a girl or when a girl walks up to them in a room and speaks to them personally.

The moments that are likely to be embarrassing occur immediately after an introduction to a person about whom you know nothing. What to say, especially if you are left alone with him and he is mute! (The person who introduces you should give you a clue, but often he doesn't. When *you* introduce two strangers, get them started off well by mentioning something about each of them.) It's usually helpful to ask a question or two. "Are you visiting in our town?" "Did Bob say you come from Dayton? I've never been to Dayton. Do you go to high school there?"

"Have you been at school long?"

"I hope you're having a good time at our party."

Acknowledging introductions to strangers calls for some quick thinking and resourcefulness. With a little practice, you will acquire skill.

Leave-taking after an introduction may be awkward too. If the conversation has been a short one, you may say simply, "Good-by, Mr. Blake, I'm glad to have met you." Or, to a young person of your own age, "Good-by, Mary, I hope you enjoy the party." Once again, simplicity and sincerity will see you through.

In all situations where questions of etiquette are involved, you will never be far off base if you remain—whether or not you know all the rules—quietly composed and if you do and say the considerate thing.

9

Living with the Family

"My parents don't understand me."

"Mother treats me like a baby."

"Everybody wants to look at a different TV program."

"I don't have any privacy."

"I think I should have the car on Saturday nights."

"My folks are too old fashioned."

"I have to take my sister along, and she tells everything!"

Are any of these complaints ever heard around your house? If not, your family is in the fortunate minority, for these gripes give expression to a few of the more common conflicts that modern living has brought to family life, and there are many more—dates, door keys, friends, late hours, school marks, young brothers and sisters, allowances, household duties. As a matter of fact, it would be hard to prove from the general atmosphere in some homes that the family group is the most all-round satisfactory way of life that mankind has devised in all his history. But that's the fact, nevertheless. Would you prefer a tribe, or a clan, or a communal village of some kind, with a head man and a council to make decisions? Of course not. That's why civilized people discarded those ways of life long ago and settled for the family setup.

So there must be more to this family way of life than discipline and arguments. Down through the ages family life must have got its reputation through harmony and co-operation, for without these the family could not function, at least successfully enough to build a reputation as the best system of life for mankind. Have our modern families got off the track somewhere along the line?

We have said that modern living is partly responsible for some family conflicts. Grandmother didn't have to make any compromises with the family on TV programs, although it is possible that Grandfather had to bargain for the horse and buggy on courting nights.

Recreation in earlier generations was largely home-centered. Houses were roomier, crowded-apartment living unknown, and the young people in the family took their household chores more or less for granted because they were not conditioned to push-button, laborsaving gadgets and appliances. We have more freedom than our grandparents had as young folks too. Modern education puts great emphasis on freedom of choice and gives us plenty of leeway in decision-making. Whether you realize it or not, in most areas of your life you have more liberty than any generation before you, and of course boys and girls in America have more personal freedom than any group of young people in the world. This too creates situations leading to family disagreements when somebody wants to apply a few rules.

But family conflicts are not the result of modern living alone. Some types have always been around and probably always will be, just as long as different personalities live together under one roof. The point is, it seems that we ought to be able to put our modern knowledge to work in areas of human relationships as well as in technology. Can't we be as smart at settling family problems as we are at repairing and creating material things? Let's make a try right now.

Some of our gripes sound pretty silly when printed in a book. But it isn't at all funny when you discover that Sally has borrowed your new sweater and stretched it, or when Dad just can't seem to understand that you can't take a girl to the Drive-In and then for a snack, and get both your date and yourself home by midnight. So what to do? Here's where our modern education may come in, if we tackle our problem with intelligence.

If you were to list all your family disagreements and try to classify them in terms of your emotional needs, you probably could group them under three needs: independence, understanding, co-operation. Aren't these the things you want most in your home and from your family? And you may be sure that every other member of the family, including even Mother and Dad, want the same things, in appropriate amounts. When you don't get them, you are frustrated, unhappy, and quarrelsome. Read the above list of complaints again and add more of your own. Don't all of them arise because you want more independence or understanding or co-operation from other members of the family? Let's take up these three needs and the troubles that arise from them.

As a sort of introduction—and to help us to stand off and look at ourselves and our family objectively, just as though it were some other family—we shall first give our family its due, so to speak. Face up to it honestly and list everything that living in a family group does for you on the favorable side. What do you get from your home? What needs does the normal home fill?

Physical needs: shelter, protection, food, clothes, medical care, and often many luxuries

Emotional needs: love, acceptance, a sense of "belonging," group living, encouragement, loyalty, guidance, discipline

Intellectual needs: education, rules of behavior, skills

Perhaps your own home supplies even more than these basic necessities for a satisfying home. Or possibly your home does not or cannot have them all. We will tackle these last situations later, but just now we have the average normal home in mind.

First, it supplies all your physical needs. Dad and Mother have dedicated their lives to this job, and they have probably been pretty successful at it. But it wasn't or isn't easy. You never realize what it means to earn a living for a family and to give them the advantages you have had until you undertake to do it yourself, because Dad and Mother don't usually gripe about it. That's the job they willingly undertook, and they are doing it with a minimum of complaint, if any.

Next to the basic necessities of life, nothing is so important to you now or to your background in later life as the love, security, and companionship that you get in your home. In other words, your emotional needs are met there. If you have had these blessings all your life, you probably take them for granted. Only someone who never had them or who has lost them can tell you what they mean to you. Even Sally's most annoying habit of borrowing your clothes or Dad's frowning disapproval of (to him) late hours shrink in importance when you contemplate how bleak life would become without Sally or Dad. So it will help us to remember, when family tensions mount, how precious that family with all its faults really is. Even though you may at times quarrel, you are learning within the family circle to give and take, to co-operate, and to share. Good sportsmanship is a trait acquired first through family living. You are acquiring it right now, or if you aren't, you had better make this your next project! The young person who goes out into life expecting to do his share, to co-operate with his fellow workers, to accept honest criticism, to make reasonable adjustments to other people, has a big start over the fellow or girl who has to develop these attitudes the hard way, outside the family. Never underestimate the importance of family life to your personal success, and never forget or ignore all that your family does for you just because they are a family. Without the background they supply, you would be tremendously handicapped later on.

Now since the family meets these emotional needs for you, let's put the shoe on the other foot. *You* are the source of supply for some of the emotional needs of the other members of your family. Dad needs your appreciation. Mother needs your sympathy. Sister needs your loyalty. Brother needs your praise. The younger children need your guidance. And they all need your love. See how it works? A family is an intricate design, with every member making his unique contribution to its beauty and utility.

Finally, from the day you first learned how to hold your own spoon, you have been acquiring all sorts of knowledge and skills from your family. Come to think of it, it takes a lot of everyday skill to get along in this world, even at an early age. Mother teaches you all the elementary skills of childhood, from how to tell time to minding your manners.

Later, your parents are concerned about your school marks because they want very much to see you properly prepared for future life with the best education they can afford to give you. They try, in other words, to meet your educational needs.

When you see them put down in print like this, the family's contributions to your life and yours to theirs begin to stand out, even to sparkle a bit.

Continuing to be intelligently objective in this family problem-solving, let's take the next step and consider what your parents have a right to expect from *you*. We are still on the family's side, you see. We'll come over to your side soon.

Are the following demands or requests reasonable? They were taken from actual statements of parents on the subject, "What I expect from my children."

Appreciation and consideration. They did not say so, but parents would be mighty pleased to receive some verbal expressions of appreciation on occasions. They surely have a right to some consideration from the family in matters of preference in TV programs, regular hours for meals, care with the family finances in the way of watching the electric lights, telephone calls, gas for the car, etc.

Some time and attention. How many fellows ever take their mothers out on a date? How many girls take an interest in mothers' clothes and hairdos? And how many of both fellows and girls plan to "visit" at home with the family some night?

Obedience. Most of the parents polled stated that they appreciated obedience in the sense that their sons and daughters did the things they knew they should do even when parents were not around to tell them, or refrained from doing wrong when their parents were not present to forbid them directly. In other words, they wanted their children to understand why certain rules were made and not to feel driven to obedience.

Some responsibility for the home. This covers about all your outside activities—good work in school, courteous manners, building a good reputation through right companions, and proper behavior.

Very likely you could add to this list because of certain situations and conditions that exist within your own family. But you would agree that these are all reasonable and are certainly the minimum "rights" of Mother and Dad.

In tackling problems that arise within the family, first you must make sure that you have done your part and have cheerfully granted your parents the rights and privileges due them. That's the first step in family arbitration. As a matter of fact, with one or two exceptions, you could almost sign that parent list of "rights" yourself. You would probably substitute "independence" for obedience and make another change or two; but if you got co-operation, loyalty, and attention from all the members of your family, you would probably think all your family problems were solved.

Assuming that your score is high on the co-operation with parents and you still are plagued with annoying or even more serious family situations, what to do?

Young people who have worked out this problem have come up with two general areas of approach to its solution, and both have been effective. The choice of method depends upon the nature of your problem.

First approach. Through your own individual efforts, which involve (1) checking your own personal attitudes, (2) thinking the problem through in its proper perspective, (3) planning for action without help from anybody.

Second approach. Through family consultation, compromise, and agreement. Some of your problems must be settled this way, if at all. There is no other course.

We shall follow the first and then the second approach through, with typical family conflicts. With some variation you can apply this approach to most family difficulties.

Bill's younger sister is the bane of his life. She is eleven and Bill is sixteen. Bill complains that Janie tattles about his dates, embarrasses him before his pals and the grownups, always wants to tag along, snoops around his room, forgets to deliver telephone messages, and is a general pest. Now let's assume that Bill is right. Janie is the typical young-sister variety of nuisance. Sometimes it's a young brother, but the effect is the same. Bill thinks that the family takes his annoyance as a joke, that if anything, they spoil Janie.

In Bill's situation, or any situation similar to it involving younger, or even sometimes older, members of the family, Approach No. 1 is called for. The first thing for Bill to tackle is his own personal attitude toward Janie and her tricks. He will have to be grown up enough himself to do a sudden switch-about and substitute for impatience, threats, complaints, and anger, some tolerance, good humor, and understanding. His other weapons have failed, so he will have to try a new type. Bill will also have to try to ignore as much of Janie's behavior as is humanly possible, and he will do well to make sure that he is not, by his own attitude, leaving his defenses down for Janie's childish attacks. She would be nonplussed if Bill suddenly assumed a big-brother attitude and paid little or no attention to her childish behavior.

Second, Bill needs to think through his problem intelligently. If he does, he will conclude that Janie behaves as she does in order to meet some of her own emotional needs. She wants attention; she may be jealous; she resents not having the freedom that her older brother has; she wants fun, which she creates at

Bill's expense; and she wants to grow up to his group—to belong. Bill would probably be very much surprised to know how often, when he is not around, Janie boasts about "my brother Bill."

These feelings of antagonism between brother and sister are not uncommon, and they are rarely deeply hostile. Most families outgrow them, but Bill can solve his problem right now if he is willing to do something beside scold and demand that Mother tell Janie where to get off.

Bill's plan for action should be clear, since it must involve meeting those emotional needs of his younger sister. She wants some of his time and attention, so Bill should see that she gets it by taking Janie to a movie now and then, by showing her how to improve her swimming stroke, by teaching her to play tennis, by helping with her homework, and by showing some interest in her school affairs. This is the way to transform Janie from an annoying nuisance into a loyal friend. It will take a little time and some planning on Bill's part; but if his complaint is as serious to him as he claims, he should, as the older one involved, be willing to work it out. And incidentally, within a few years, the gap between Bill and his sister will begin to close, for Janie will have become a young lady. Then a happy relationship will mean much to both. There is something very special about a harmonious brother-sister friendship.

Betty's problem is quite different from Bill's, but just as common. She wants more freedom and independence, but her mother treats her about as she did when Betty was ten. She selects Betty's clothes, objects to her use of lipstick, says Betty at fifteen is too young to have dates, and generally tries to run Betty's life for her.

Approach No. 1 will help Betty too, for she, like Bill, should stand off and observe her own attitude. She needs to demonstrate to her mother that she really is a young lady and is ready to assume new responsibilities and take the consequences of the choices she makes "on her own." One way *not* to convince Mother of this is to resort to childish attitudes and behavior: to pout, cry, coax, sulk, or get angry and stubborn. Betty will appear as grown up as she wants to be considered if she remains calm, reasonable, understanding; admits a few things, such as, that too much lipstick might be unattractive; or asks Mother's advice about clothes; and suggests a foursome instead of a twosome for dates. With Betty behaving like a grownup, it won't be long before Mother remarks to Dad, "You know, Betty seems to have grown up over night."

If Betty thinks her problem through, she will realize that Mother, who has been looking after Betty for all her fifteen years, still feels responsible for her, which she is in fact—to the community and to the law.

You probably have heard too many times some such statement as "I only want what is for your own good." But it is nevertheless true that your good is exactly what your parents do want. Would you like it any other way? It would be infinitely worse not to have anyone feel responsible for you, even though you may feel Mom and Dad are overplaying the act at this point in your life. Complete independence could be pretty terrifying. You, like Betty, not only need but also *want* a definite amount of protection, security, and limitations to your freedom. All young people do. You know how confused, unhappy, and out of tune are fellows and girls who have received no discipline, or too little, from their homes.

But there are things Betty and others in her situation can do to loosen those apron strings a bit. Her plan for action has been suggested above. Instead of coaxing and arguing, Betty will help both herself and her mother if she begins to assume complete responsibility, without prompting, for some areas of her life—her room, for example, and her clothes (which means Mother doesn't have to iron a blouse in a rush some morning); if she is faithful to her school work and discusses school and other interests with her mother; if she always keeps her promises; and if she is sympathetic with Mother's concern for the entire household. In brief, if Betty can become a partner with Mother, she will shortly acquire more independence. Without Mother's realizing it herself, her attitude toward Betty will change.

Joe is frankly not a student. Academic ability is just not his dish. So he wants to quit school at sixteen and get a job. But Dad is firm about Joe's getting the education he himself was denied. Dad knows only too well the struggle that a person has getting ahead today without adequate schooling. To make it even more difficult for Joe, the family finances are inadequate to meet the needs of a growing family, and Joe wants to help out.

Joe cannot work this problem out by himself. There are too many people involved, so Approach No. 2 should help. This involves consultation among those concerned and some mutually satisfactory compromise reached if possible.

If Joe's parents will agree to it, it would be profitable for them to sit down with Joe and his principal, or with the school counselor or other teacher in whom they have confidence, and talk this problem through. If Joe were a student and had intellectual ambitions, which means that he could head for a profession or other lifework calling for advanced study, his problem would be worked out one way. It would involve making plans for Joe to complete high school and get to college. But Joe is not headed for college. Even so, his educational advisers will probably point out to him that a high-school diploma, even with below average grades, will be of enormous benefit to him, not only in getting a job, but also in higher earning power and in personal development. When, around a conference table or in the principal's office, Dad and Mother have their say, Joe expresses himself frankly, and the principal or teacher speaks from his experience and his knowledge of Joe and his work, the problem itself will seem smaller. It always helps to pull things out into the open and discuss them thoroughly. Joe will learn something and so will his parents. They may agree that the best course for Joe is a school-job setup—if this arrangement is possible in the local school system—whereby Joe can get a job and learn a business or trade while he continues to pursue certain school courses.

If your problem is the same or similar to Joe's, remember that no young person ever profits in the long run from quitting school. And if the disagreement is centered around college, try the same sort of compromise. There are colleges and universities, mostly in the large cities or state universities, where students can advance in a business or some form of creative work while working for their degrees.

There is another very common area of disagreement and family dispute which involves both the young men and the girls of the family. This is the general question of frequency of dates, hours kept, use of the family car, week-end trips, and all the other situations that arise when young people are old enough to have some social life among themselves.

"Everybody is going, why can't I?" "All the kids drive out to Hamburger Heaven after the dance." "Twelve o'clock is too early to break up the party." "Chaperons are old fashioned." "I think I should have the car one night a week." These are familiar complaints in many homes.

A combination of the two approaches to problems may be necessary in settling these questions of young people's social life. It helps a great deal to understand that our parents realize, even though they may not be able to make it clear to you, that the years between twelve and eighteen are the most important in your life as far as your development is concerned. Habits acquired now, stick. Your most important decisions are made now —the kind of education you will acquire, very often the vocation you will enter, your preparation for marriage, your religious faith, your reputation in the community and among your friends and adult acquaintances—to mention a few. It is little wonder, then, that your parents find it so hard to stand by and let you make serious mistakes in choices or develop unwholesome attitudes and habits. Be very sure, before you rebel against parental advice or authority, that Dad and Mother are wrong.

Next, if these complaints are common among the young people and the parents of your community, get together and set up a code that both sides promise to live up to.

For example, in one community a group of fellows and girls went to the president of the local Parent-Teacher Association and asked her to arrange for an open meeting where representatives of parents, teachers, and students could conduct a panel and build such a code. Even lacking a P.T.A. you can do the same thing through your church, a local service club like the Rotary or Kiwanis, or your school. Everyone involved will get the other fellow's point of view, parents will also know just what course other families are taking, and all will settle on satisfactory rules and regulations based on the community situation and on what is practical and reasonable.

Then it is up to the young people to come through. Bob will wash and polish the car and be a safe driver. Betty and her date will be home at the promised hour, and the hour agreed upon will depend upon the nature of the date. No one expects to be home from the Junior Prom as early as from a Saturday night movie. And Dad and Mother will be in the plan too.

There are many "gadgets" that make family life smoother by eliminating minor irritations. These include a family bulletin board for posting telephone messages, meal hours, special family duties to remember, and so on. In some families the television set has created such a situation that they have drawn up definite schedules for everybody's viewing pleasure. If living space is small, families have to co-operate by sharing closets and drawer space. Two sisters rooming together can help each other out and avoid friction if they create some semblance of privacy for one another, even to hooks and hangers. If all this sounds pretty silly to you in connection with your home life, remind yourself that business offices employ just such methodical schemes for helping people work together in harmony. Employers consider these schemes efficient. Many homes would be happier and more pleasant if they borrowed a few of the methods of business and added to them all the advantages that families have over business—love, affection, fun that is shared, close family ties, and the wonderful privilege of growing up together.

10

Homework

By "homework" we do not mean doing the dishes or mowing the lawn. We have in mind that "battle of the books"—in other words, school assignments.

If studying is a pleasure and you have little trouble making acceptable marks, you are one of the lucky ones. Even so, you want to be sure that you know where you are headed and what A's and B's on your report card mean in terms of real life. High marks are not worth much for themselves alone. The work and knowledge that they reflect must be coupled with a lot of other things for the long haul on the road to success. The brightest student must also have a sound character, good health, courage, and common sense, to mention a few of the essential qualities for successful living.

For the student who has a tougher time with science and math and languages, it is encouraging to remember how high your all-round score in life can be if you have the qualities just mentioned. Personality, the ability to keep your head, reliability, and other qualities that you either have or can acquire will help you make good in some line of work for which you are suited, as well as in all other life relationships. So do not be discouraged because school is difficult. There may be ways of getting on top of some of that homework if you are serious about trying. Let's look at some ideas that have worked for other average or below-average students.

Brilliant or just average, every young person should understand, first of all, what education is all about.

"I don't know why I have to take algebra. I'll never use it!" moans one young lady, while across the aisle a boy complains, "How will French help me get a job?" And somebody else chimes in, "I can't remember history, and who cares about those old kings anyway?"

Obviously, some high-schoolers do not know why they are studying, what they are studying, or what the real purpose of education is. About one out of every four Americans is attending some kind of school this year. So there must be some reason for education's popularity. What is it?

Of course, everybody knows that more and more employers are demanding at least a high-school education for jobs that involve more than unskilled labor. But the hours that you are spending on English, French, science, history, or any other subject of the school curriculum have far more value for you than simply steppingstones to a job. Actually, you are working on those blueprints that we have been thinking about. As you tackle your homework each day, you are building a life that will bring you happiness, lasting satisfactions, and genuine success, because your education goes far beyond the subjects you are studying, important as these are.

First, you are learning to *try*. All of life's experiences—whether you are earning your living, keeping house in that dream home, engaging in athletics, doing something creative, serving on a committee, or anything else you can think of that is worth while—involve effort, sometimes a great deal of effort, and if you are not learning in school to walk up to a task, difficult or unpleasant, and try hard, you will have a rough time of it later on. Others will go ahead, while you are using up mental and emotional energy trying to break the bad habit you have acquired of ducking a job or playing around with it halfheartedly. Your education will teach you to *try,* and this is half your battle in any area of life.

Second, you are learning to *concentrate.* You know better than anybody else how easy it is to daydream when you are supposed to be studying about the Articles of Confederation or the Bill of Rights. Maybe it's even harder to keep your mind on a Latin declension or the neutralization of bases and acids. But it's a funny thing about the habit of concentration. If it is not cultivated, in time it becomes just as difficult to concentrate on something in which you are very much interested as on something you find dull. Learning a musical score, figuring out a dress pattern, playing chess, flying a plane, keeping a job, and everything else that is worth while takes a heap of concentration. You will be a flunky at many things if your education has not taught you to concentrate.

Third, you are learning to enjoy and get the most from this amazing world in which we live. It is a great tragedy that millions of people are denied the most thrilling of life's experiences because their senses are dull. They are blind and deaf to great music, to the wonders of science, to the magic of the written word, to the beauty of nature, even to the interesting people and events around them. They have never been taught to appreciate the best, so they settle for the shoddy, the second rate, the phony imitation of the real thing. To be sure, most of them never know what they are missing, but that does not make their stunted lives any the less tragic. A mole is content to burrow through the ground, sightless, but who would not rather be a bird? The books you are studying today, in whatever subjects, are making your mind keener and your interests broader, if you see to it that they serve you. Every year of your life you will discover more and more interesting facts about the world in which you live, and you will enjoy more and more thrilling experiences because your study has taught you *appreciation* of all that is worth while.

Fourth, you are learning to be versatile and adaptable. Today there are too many lopsided specialists who, if their one line of endeavor is removed, get fearful or think they are helpless. For example, the serious study of science is important and necessary and it requires, in its advanced stages, most of a student's time and effort. But the graduates of one of the best-known technical colleges in the world have recently made public complaint about their one-sided education. They realize they have missed a lot on the way up, for both their personal development and their jobs. If positions in the field of science become more difficult to find than they are today, where will they turn?

These students would tell you that French literature can do something for you that chemistry cannot do, that algebra can give you something that history cannot, that music may be just as valuable to you as woodworking, and so on. They would say that because in college or on the job you will have to specialize, it is important that you take advantage of high-school days to delve into as many different courses of study as you can and to learn to use both your head and your hands in intellectual, artistic, and practical ways. American high schools offer unusual opportunity for such variety if a student is interested enough to take advantage of it.

Fifth, you are acquiring *knowledge* and *skills*. For some of you, high school will be the end of your formal education. It does not take fellows and girls who leave school early very long to discover that their prospects for any kind of challenging job are seriously limited. If they found school difficult or boring or confining, they have found the kind of jobs they are capable of filling without education infinitely more difficult and boring and confining. That is why night schools and part-time schools are crammed with young people. They muffed their first chance, and now they have to work harder, often after a day on the regular job. Let your education prepare you with those knowledges and skills which will enable you to earn a living, to be resourceful when necessary, and to be able to stand on your own feet if that responsibility should arise sooner than you expect.

Education, you see, goes far beyond "book learning." If it consisted only of cramming one's mind full of facts and memorizing certain processes, you might have reason to complain and drop those subjects that you find difficult or uninteresting. But remembering education's far-reaching importance and effects, it pays every young man and woman to stay in school as long as possible and take advantage of what is probably the best system of public education in the world, certainly the most comprehensive—namely, our American public schools.

It is not reasonable to expect that all studies will be equally interesting to you, but if schoolwork is difficult, here are some tips that have proved helpful to many students. When you some day find a job, you will expect to learn to do your work in the most efficient way possible. School is your job at the moment.

There are right and wrong ways to study, just as there are right and wrong ways of tackling any job. Maybe you have been muddling along with your homework without planning or using efficient methods, and consequently your marks look about as sick as you feel about the whole business.

So, first, what about the *mechanics* of studying—your tools and equipment? Here they are, and if you are really in earnest about doing better school work, these will help you.

1. Make a written record of each assignment, as it is given out by your teacher. Have a notebook for these records. Don't get into the habit of telephoning a pal after school, probably at night when you finally get around to homework, to find out what history or math or something else is due for the next day. That's one way to waste fifteen minutes while you talk about a lot of other things in addition to the assignment. And don't jot down the assignments on scraps of paper that are easily mislaid. The fact that you have an orderly record of assignments when you settle down to study will make you *feel* more successful to start with.

2. Prepare a study schedule of time, place, and subject—and stick to it. The time should *not* be after you have done everything else that you want to do. Remember, school is your *job;* you would not dream of trying to fill a job for an employer after you had finished all your social duties. So don't cheat yourself on your present job, which also is bringing you big returns.

The place you study may be almost anywhere, as long as you are alone and physically comfortable. And no radio, TV or family present. There is something about having a regular place for study that in itself gets you into the mood for studying. In time, your mind associates that particular spot with concentration and study.

Your study schedule will be fitted into your home duties, extracurricular school activities, church affairs, and so on. All these are important and part of your education too, but be efficient and keep every activity in its rightful place. If school subjects are difficult, you may have to forgo other activities in their favor. And it will be worth it to you. Take pencil and paper, or preferably a page of your assignment notebook, and make up a time schedule for the week. This can include any special dates you may have in addition to your study schedule. Assign the most study time, of course, to the most difficult subject. During your study time at school, prepare for those subjects that require library or other reference work not possible at home.

3. Keep your study tools (except books and notebooks that you have to carry to school) in your place for study—*always*. These will include well-sharpened pencils, a pen, plenty of paper, a dictionary, and any other equipment that special subjects may require.

So far so good. Now for your state of mind, and this is important, particularly if you have not been doing work that is satisfactory either to your teachers or to yourself. First, have confidence in yourself. The fact that some courses are difficult, or even that you have to work harder on all of them than some of your classmates seem to, does not mean that you are a dimwit. You have your strong points, so believe in yourself.

Then, accept the fact that study takes time. There are no shortcuts or substitutes for time and serious effort. This is just as true, even more so, for the most brilliant scientist you could mention as it is for you. How long did it take you to learn to swim, or play chess, or handle some musical instrument with skill? Schoolwork takes time too.

You will be helped enormously if you cultivate certain classroom habits. You may have to work at this, but you cannot succeed without them. Here they are:

1. Have the right books and materials with you when you get to class. More planning, you see. The poor student is likely to be the one who forgets notebooks, laboratory manuals, even the right book sometimes. He never gets himself organized.

2. Learn to listen to what is going on, including what your teacher is saying! And take notes too of anything that may help when you are at home studying by yourself. Forget the date you had last night or the one you hope to have next Saturday. Don't let your attention wander to Bob's new sweater, or to Phil's latest gimmick for amusing himself, or to the world outside the window. Concentrate on your job.

3. Take part in classroom discussions. You don't have to be an "eager beaver" to do your share in helping through class participation to make a subject stick, for yourself as well as others. The student who sits back, either without interest or through shyness, is likely to have trouble with his studies.

4. Don't be afraid to ask questions. If you feel you have too many questions to ask, you may want to postpone some to raise with the teacher alone. But you must be sure you understand the points made, or you will get behind in your work.

With this preparation, what can you do when you actually open those books for study? Your procedure will depend somewhat upon the nature of the particular subject. Mathematics requires one kind of approach, history another, and so on. But in general, try to follow these suggestions or adapt them to your needs:

1. Read your assignment carefully. Pick out what seem to be the important points. If the narrative is lengthy, as in history, civics, or the like, outline the content of the chapter.

2. Look over the notes you took in class. Did the teacher make any special suggestions or requests? Did he explain any-

thing that you would find in your study? Your notes should include these.

3. Review quickly, if you do not need to spend too much time, what you have been over before in this particular subject.

4. Read the assignment again and check your grasp of it with any questions that appear in the book.

If the assignment calls for written work, problem-solving, etc., make sure you understand exactly what is called for. Do you understand how to do the problem? If not, review your text. If the textbook gives you a problem, you may be sure that you have been told somewhere in that text how to do it. Look in the index to your book for page references to terms you do not understand; then go back to learn those terms, processes, and so on. If you have not been doing this and are behind in the course, you will have to put in extra time and effort to catch up. Your experience demonstrates how important it is to you to begin the first day of the school year to keep on schedule with your studying and learn each day's lesson well.

And speaking of the index to your book, be sure you make good use of that textbook. It is your most important tool and contains many things for your aid that some students ignore and therefore lose valuable help. Read the introductions to chapters, and the reviews of chapters which are often provided. Use the pictures, graphs, and charts to make points clear to you. That is why they are there. Be sure to check yourself with any questions in the text. If you can answer these, you have grasped the day's lesson. If you cannot answer them, yon need more study, so turn back to check on the answers you could not give.

Always read and study your textbook for *ideas,* not words. What is the author saying to you about equations, chemicals, literature, some period of the world's history?

If your assignment is a written one, calling for paragraphs of narrative, write it out on scrap paper. Then check it carefully for spelling, grammar, and punctuation before you make your final copy. Yes, all this takes time. So will every job you get.

If languages do not come easy to you, try writing out on small cards some French or Spanish phrases. Carry the cards around in your bag or pocket and take a peak at them at odd moments anywhere, on the bus, walking to school, going on errands. Do the same with principles of grammar that you have to learn, in English or any other language.

All these suggestions and tips will help you enormously if you are really sincere about wanting to improve your schoolwork. And finally, reward yourself for some study accomplishment. If you want to hear some special television program, promise yourself to complete your science lesson first and immediately carry that promise out. But don't cheat and hurry through the lesson superficially. Or if you want to do something very special on Saturday afternoon, make a serious bargain with yourself to go, provided you get your math done or that English theme written.

Cheating is so common in high schools these days that the practice is accepted as casually as any prevailing fashion would be. That is a great pity, for cheating accomplishes nothing except to get you, perhaps, an occasional higher mark and to make a dishonest person out of you. One has to get used to cheating. When you cheat for the first time, you feel guilty and unhappy about it. Then, gradually, conscience is dulled and a pattern—a habit, if you will—of dishonesty sets in.

Young people are tempted to cheat largely because of the emphasis that teachers and parents put upon grades, or marks. Marks do not mean a thing unless they represent what you have learned. And if you get 90 on a math paper because you copied somebody else's work, you have flunked just as completely as though you had done your own work and received 50, because 50 represented what you really knew, based on your own study.

It is smart to do the best work of which you are capable, and not to worry about marks, at least to the point at which you are driven to cheating to attain them. Life will ask what you have in your head. Your job will demand intelligence, accuracy, a good memory, an analytical mind—several or all of these qualities, and cheating to compensate for neglect of your homework, or to get higher grades than you deserve, won't see you through over the long pull.

No matter how hard you have to work or how pressing the need is for you to get a full-time job and help out financially at home, think a long time before you quit school. The fellow and girl who at least finish high school, get all the breaks vocationally. They get better wages, they are hired first and have more job security, they do more interesting work, with more possibility for promotion. Even though you quit school with the idea that you will complete your education "some day," statistics prove that you will probably never do so. You will lose the habit for study, you will be too tired or too engrossed in other things to sustain your ambition for more education, or you will just not care.

So plan intelligently to get on top of that homework. You will never again, throughout your entire life, get what you can get in school.

11

Careers Ahead

WHETHER YOU ARE TO GO ON TO college after high school or your formal education will come to an end with the high-school diploma, it is necessary, or at least desirable, for you to begin to think about the kind of lifework you hope to enter.

There are several reasons for this. In the first place, the courses you elect to take in high school should be along the lines of your chosen occupation. Otherwise you may have to do some serious readjusting and extra work the last year of high school, if that is possible, or you may have to spend another year in postgraduate study to meet the entrance requirements of the college you finally decide to attend. You should have some rather definite idea as to whether you want to enter one of the professions—in which case college is a must—whether your object is business, some highly skilled trade, some form of creative art, or a similar category of interest.

Not only will your choice have some bearing on your high school subjects, but it will also direct you to outside activities that will be helpful to you: the debating society, the musical organizations, the school paper, some extracurricular task that needs your clever hands, some form of record-keeping, or an administrative assignment.

If, however, you have no ideas about what you want for a lifework, do not worry about it. Few young people of your age have. But the purpose of this chapter is to give you some pointers on how you may find what is the most suitable career for you.

The first thing you want to think about is the question, "What do I want from my vocation?" If you think about this very seriously, you will probably come up with something like the following answers. These are not listed necessarily in the order of their importance.

"I want job satisfaction." That is, you want to feel at the end of a day's work, or of a year's work, that you have made some contribution to the job, to your place or position of employment, and thus to yourself. You do not want to be bored or kicked around or feel useless.

"I want adequate wages." Granted that "money isn't everything," you have a right to expect from your labor fair compensation for what your education, training, and experience bring to that job.

"I want to keep on learning." This may be a question of learning more and more about the work you are doing, keeping abreast of new developments, or creating worth-while byproducts to your job. It is not difficult; in fact, it is necessary that the doctor, nurse, teacher, and other professional person, as well as a business person, learn more and more on their job. But it is sometimes not possible for the industrial worker engaged in a purely routine job to do this. So such a worker must make an effort to use his leisure time in such a way that he will grow—mentally, socially, and spiritually. We shall have more suggestions to make about this later.

"I want to make some contribution to the world." There are many vocations, sometimes highly remunerative in terms of money, that contribute to the ill-being rather than the well-being of the world. Your time, your energy, your precious life must not be ruined in such an enterprise. Your vocation may be concerned with such everyday things as automobiles or textiles or food products; all of us cannot be ministers or teachers or doctors or nurses, who contribute *directly* to the spiritual and social needs of others. But your career, if wisely chosen and conscientiously followed, will serve the world.

Your final statement may be, "I want a job for which I am suited." You don't want to be a round peg in a square hole. There are far too many girls in business offices, for example, who should be working with children or engaged in some other vocation for which they obviously have aptitudes. There are too many stockbrokers who would have made skillful engineers or landscape gardeners. And so on, and so on. The wrong choice of vocation causes more restlessness, fatigue, and even physical illness than hard work ever does. How can you find *your* career?

First, discover for yourself what kind of person you are mentally. If your high school grades are fairly satisfactory or are above average, the chances are that you can make good in any vocation that interests you, including those professions that demand a good mind and a liking for study. There is one thing sure, if school work is really hard (and not just the result of your laziness or indifference) you probably should not try to secure the necessary education for any of the professions. All of them demand long and stiff sessions with books.

What kind of person are you socially? Do you like to meet people, and can you talk with them rather easily, or would you like to cultivate this skill? Have you a sound sense of humor, emotional stability, patience, and a good nature? If so, even though your school grades were never high or even a good average, you may be a highly successful sales person, you may have just the touch needed to work successfully with people in one of several kinds of commercial agencies, you may be adept at food preparation, you can earn your living at one of the highly skilled trades. All of these attract the sociable person, who gets along well with people and can sell products or services successfully.

What are your interests and aptitudes? Look through the following list of job families, with your occupational future in mind. Does any one of them ring a bell?

Artistic	Farming	Personal service
Child care	General clerical	Public contact
Computing	Literary	Public service
Cooking	Managerial	Record-keeping
Entertainment	Musical	Technical

These job families are concerned with the skills, talents, and interests of an individual, not with a definite job or profession within the job family. There are many different occupations within each family. The managerial job, for example, may be within an industry, in a store, at some outdoor occupation, and so on. But the point is, the manager must have managerial ability, which he puts to work wherever he finds the opportunity.

Are you mechanically inclined? Do you enjoy and are you patient with children? Do you like books? Are you interested in writing or music or medicine? Do you like to debate—and to prepare through hard study for debate? Do you speak well? Do you like to sew, cook, design? What are your favorite studies? Your hobbies? Your social activities?

These are some of the questions you must ask as you study yourself. They are broken down further in books on vocational guidance which you will find listed in the Source Books.

You will find other possible interests as you study the wide range of occupations open to you today. Think about all the trades, businesses, and professions carried on in your own community. Talk with adult workers about their jobs. Read through current magazines with your future occupation in mind. Many of them have vocational guidance departments. Talk with your teachers and school counselor. Think about the many new fields in the modern world: television and the many kinds of repair services needed to care for modern equipment; the various branches of medicine and nursing, such as therapeutic work and public health; the interesting fields of cookery; the vast range of science; the occupations open in the fields of marketing, display, packaging, advertising. Your occupational choice is almost limitless.

A few words of caution. Avoid fields that are likely to be overcrowded, unless you are sure you can meet keen competition.

Give serious thought to the demands a given occupation will make upon you. Have you the robust health required? Will you be happy in the community in which you will have to locate? Will your chosen career call for some financial investment, a long period of apprenticeship, more education and training than you have the time and money to spend?

Think about the stability of the occupation too. Is it one that depends upon periods of prosperity and luxury-spending? These are the first to "fold" when times get hard. Is it an occupation that demands youth and physical vigor? In other words, can you still make a living in the field when you are fifty and past?

Finally, do not be a job snob. That is to say, do not enter a vocational field because of its so-called prestige, if you do not honestly feel called to it. A white collar can be a chain around your neck if you are bored with it and interested in little except clean hands and your pay check. You might be wonderfully happy wearing work clothes as you work with tools.

In addition to reading and learning about jobs through hearsay, there are practical ways in which you can discover your interests and aptitudes. One is through part-time work during vacation periods or possibly after school, if you do not sacrifice your schoolwork for the job. Working in a store will give you a rather definite idea of how you would make out in a merchandising job. Even baby-sitting shows up your skill and patience, or lack of them, with children. Changing tires and doing odd jobs around a garage will demonstrate that you like mechanics and selling services to the public or that such a job is not for you. Working in an office may interest you. Working on a farm may attract you permanently to that way of life or bore you. While you are in school, you may have to take whatever job you can find, if you need one, but keep your eyes and ears open to learn all you can about areas of work.

Another possibility for gaining knowledge and experience is to help out in community institutions or projects. Working as a junior aid in a hospital will attract you to some form of nursing career or send you scurrying away in a hurry. Church activities will call forth your qualities of leadership or your equally valuable qualities of intelligent "followership." Public recreation may prove to be your calling, and that field is wide today.

Hobbies often point the way to a career too, and do not overlook what comes easy. That may well be just the vocation for you. Photography, woodworking, writing, cooking, sewing, dancing, gardening, tinkering with any kind of tool, music, playing around with chemicals in the cellar—any one may well mean a career.

You may have a part-time job, or possibly your situation will be such that you will have a full-time job that offers little if anything in the way of stimulation or possibilities for personal growth. Perhaps even now you are denied some of the advantages that other young people in your community have. Some of the greatest people of the world have had just such experiences and have lived through just such periods as you are now having or may have later on the job. Insofar as your job is concerned, always keep the following in mind. The following suggestions came directly from young industrial workers whose jobs were boring, monotonous, and without a future. They decided, while discussing their problems in a church youth fellowship, that they could do little about their jobs, so they must tackle themselves and their *attitudes*. Here are their ideas, and they worked.

One: do your job, however boring, to perfection. There is a mental lift that results from doing a job right, even if it is turning screws all day. Your job may not be personally uplifting, but it is necessary, or you would not be paid to do it.

Two: do not waste emotional energy and get yourself tired out physically by pitying yourself or wishing you were somewhere else doing something else. If, at least for the time being, this is your job, think about pleasant, perhaps more important things, and try to be friendly and help along your fellow associates.

Three: cultivate worth-while interests outside your job. Then, without interfering with the quality of your work, you can look forward to some hobby, educational course, athletic activity, or church group.

Four: have a plan for your life which is higher than your job. Don't set your sights beyond anything you can ever hope to achieve, but consider further education, a new home, advancing with some hobby so that you become expert, joining some group to make new friends, taking up some form of music or art, however modest it may be.

All these plans served as "safety valves" to relieve drugging monotony and to smother hopeless attitudes. As these young workers suggested, in your school studies and in planning for your lifework, you are working on the blueprints for your life, and those blueprints are all-important in this area of vocational choice. To make a mistake in your career-building results in frustration, unhappiness, and the bitter experience of a misspent life. Conversely, the right career brings permanent satisfaction, material rewards, and constant growth. Begin now, while in school, to set up a goal for your life. Vocationally it need not be too definite. You may change your occupational choices several times, even after you go to work. But resolve to do your best at school, to cultivate wide interests, to take the fullest advantage of your educational opportunities. Steer your studies, your social life, your community activities, your job experience, in the direction of your highest and worthiest dreams.

SOURCE BOOKS
for Pleasure and Guidance

Titles are listed in the order of subject matter presented in the book.

Becker, May, ed. *Youth Replies, I Can.* New York: Alfred A Knopf, Inc., 1945.
Fisher, Dorothea C. *A Fair World to All.* New York: McGraw-Hill Book Co., 1952.
Kennedy, John F. *Profiles in Courage.* New York: Harper & Bros., 1956.
Anderson, Marian. *My Lord, What a Morning.* New York: The Viking Press, 1956.
Rupert, Hoover, ed. *Your Life Counts.* Nashville: Abingdon Press, 1950.
Broadbent, Adah. *Teen-age Glamor.* Garden City, N. Y. Doubleday & Co., 1955.
Pashko, Stanley. *Boy's Book of Body Building.* New York: Grosset & Dunlap, 1952.
Daly, Maureen. *Smarter and Smoother.* New York: Dodd, Mead & Co., 1944.
Carson, Byrta. *How You Look and Dress.* New York: McGraw-Hill Book Co., 1955.
Eisenberg, Helen and Larry. *Fun with Skits, Stunts and Stories.* New York: Association Press, 1955.
De Leeuw, Adèle L. *It's Fun to Cook.* New York: The Macmillan Co., 1952.
Zarchy, Harry. *Stamp Collector's Guide.* New York: Alfred A. Knopf, Inc., 1956.
Astle, Cedric. *Let's Write a Story.* London: Edmund Ward, Ltd., 1954. (Published in England, but available in many American libraries.)
Scott, Barbara Ann, and Kirby, Michael. *Skating for Beginners.* New York: Alfred A. Knopf, Inc., 1953.
Bossing, Nelson L., and Martin, Robert R. *Youth Faces Its Problems.* River Forest, Ill.: Laidlaw Brothers, 1950.
McDermott, Irene E., and Nicholas, Florence W. *Living for Young*

Moderns. Philadelphia: J. B. Lippincott Co., 1956.

Lerrigo, Marion O., and Southard, Helen F. *What's Happening to Me?* New York: E. P. Dutton & Co., 1956.

———. *Learning About Love*. New York: E. P. Dutton & Co., 1956.

Lindner, Robert M. *Must You Conform?* New York: Rinehart & Co., 1956.

Scherf, Charles H. *Do Your Own Thinking*. New York: McGraw-Hill Book Co., 1948.

Sportsmanlike Driving. Washington, D. C.: American Automobile Association, 1955.

Daly, Sheila J. *Blondes Prefer Gentlemen*. New York: Dodd, Mead & Co., 1949.

Daly, Maureen. *The Perfect Hostess*. New York: Dodd, Mead & Co., 1950.

Ulmann, Frances. *Getting Along with Brothers and Sisters*. Chicago: Science Research Associates, 1950.

Du Jardin, Rosamond. *Practically Seventeen*. Philadelphia: J. B. Lippincott Co., 1949. (Fiction; good family relationships presented.)

Wrenn, Charles G. *Practical Study Aids*. Stanford, Calif.: Stanford University Press, 1931. (Pamphlet.)

Bennett, Margaret E. *Getting the Most out of College*. New York: McGraw-Hill Book Co., 1950.

Ferrari, Erma P. *Careers for You*. Nashville: Abingdon Press, 1953.

Leeming, Joseph. *Jobs That Take You Places*. New York: David McKay Co., 1953. (Jobs for young people interested in working outside America.)

Randolph, Helen R., *et al. You and Your Life*. Boston: Houghton Mifflin Co., 1951.